Praise for
Working Hell to Workir

"Lindsay Barnett beautifully defined the duality between work and life and reminds us that we can't accept the status quo. It is time to take back control and make work, work for us. We have the power to determine just how good it can be."

—Jenni Pfaff, Music Executive and Business/Culture Transformation Expert, Warner Chappell Music

"As an employer of a growing company, and an employee myself, this book is timely and incredibly valuable. It provides practical tools for creating a culture that embraces identities and needs while still aligning towards a shared vision and mission. It also offered great tips for fostering mindfulness within each of us along with encouraging greater empathy for others."

—-Rajiv Mahadevan, CEO Attune Neurosciences and Serial Entrepreneur

"Working Hell to Working Well is a must-read for anyone seeking to break free from burnout and create a fulfilling, sustainable career. Lindsay Barnett masterfully guides readers on the journey from hustle to harmony, offering actionable strategies to redefine work-life balance, reclaim time, and build a workplace culture where well-being is the norm, not the exception."

—Melissa Karz, Partner, Next Step Partners, Author of Invisible Bridges

"P.A.U.S.E.! You may not know this acronym yet, but after reading this book, it'll become part of your daily routine. I love books that blend self-development with actionable workplace strategies, and this one delivers. With pragmatic advice and coaching, you'll have tools you can apply immediately."

—*Joseph Green, Worldwide Vice President, Netskope*

"*Working Hell to Working Well* is an engaging, thoughtful guide for navigating the balance between work and life, offering practical tools to reduce stress and reclaim time. Through her personal stories, research, and actionable advice, Barnett provides a roadmap not only for employees, but for people leaders and organizations as well to improve well-being."

—*Jennifer Sandoz, SVP Human Resources*

"Barnett embodies the principles she advocates in her book. Her dedication to creating a balanced and fulfilling work environment is not just theoretical—it's a lived experience that she shares with authenticity and passion."

—*Matt Hostetler, CHRO, Energy Recovery*

"Barnett speaks to the needs we all have to show up at work in an impactful and sustainable way. Use this book to get the clarity needed to meet the organization's priorities while also meeting your own."

— *Molly Rosen, Founder and Co-CEO of ProjectNext Leadership*

Working Hell to Working Well

Making Your Company Work for You

Lindsay K. Barnett

Working Hell to Working Well:
Making Your Company Work for You

Copyright © Lindsay K. Barnett (2025)

All rights reserved. No part of this publication may be reproduced, stored in a retrieval system, or transmitted, in any form or by any means, without the prior written permission of the publisher.

Published by:

AUTHORS on MISSION

Dedication

To the role models—past, present, and future—whose courage lights the way. You make it possible to do the best work of our lives and have our lives be our best work.

Table of Contents

Introduction

"I'm just so overwhelmed right now with work and life."

"I'm worried my team has been working nights and weekends lately, but I'm sure it will all be better soon..."

"I'm working so hard. When will my manager recognize the value I am bringing to the team?"

"My manager sends emails and texts on the weekend, so I feel like I need to respond right away."

"I want to make a change, but I just don't have enough time to even think about what that could be."

"I used to have friends and hobbies, but now it seems like all I have time for is work."

If any of the statements above resonated with you, I can assure you I have been in your shoes. After a couple of decades in the corporate world, I have seen a lot. I've grappled with finding purpose and meaning at work. I've navigated the pain points of both hypergrowth and learning to "do more with less." I've juggled the demands of work plus caregiving. I've had unsupportive bosses and toxic team members. I've balanced leading global teams with seemingly never-ending work hours across time zones. And so on, and so on...

But there has been a ton of hard-earned learning and growth along the way, particularly around finding the right flow between work and life. As an internal human resources leader for much of my career, I have observed corporate life spanning industries from advertising to biotech to consumer-packaged goods. And then corporate life stages from start-up to turnaround to stable growth. Throughout it, I have had the unique perspective of having created some of the systems and structures that intend to support employees, leaders, and organizations to perform at their best. Along with my individual coaching experience, I plan to use my bird's eye view into how organizations work to empower you to shape your employee experience. Of course, I will also share the experiences that have colored my own career journey.

As excited as I am to share my learnings with you, I also want to make sure I keep it real. Like many others, the pandemic opened my eyes to how work was going for me and a lot of the employees in the organizations that I have worked for. In my twenty-plus years in human resources, I have coached and counseled thousands of employees with the hope that they have a great experience at work. However, from my seat, I also saw a lot of the ways that people and organizations created stress and, frankly, pain in the day-to-day. That led me to the insight that if we want greater well-being in the workplace, we need to accept how we all contribute. It's not fair to put accountability just on the employee. Just as it isn't reasonable to think that leaders and organizations are solely responsible either. We all need to work together.

Once well-being is on your radar, there are some great examples out there. A couple of years ago, I was in conversation with some leaders at the World Happiness Summit[1] and we were discussing good practices we've seen. One person shared that when they head home from the office for the day, they make a habit of "leaving loudly." This usually consisted of making a good show of packing up their belongings, firmly closing the laptop, turning off their office lights, cheerily saying goodbye to people, and just about slamming the door on their way out. While I may have added a little dramatic flair here, I love how it contradicts a commonly held opposing belief that to get ahead in the workplace, you need to be the first in and the last out of the office. And in our always-on workday in recent years, that may also look like emails and texts at all hours. Anything to show how much and how hard we are working, right?

Leaving loudly, in contrast, declares there is a line between work and life, and I'm going to do the life bit now. It may take some bravery not to slither out of the office, let alone leave loudly. Yet, hearing this story, I had an a-ha moment. The more of us who truly role model how we harmonize between work and life, the less political capital or courage will be needed by us all collectively in the future. Of course, leaders and organizations play a role, too, by fostering a culture that supports our whole selves. By aligning our intentions, we can all nurture workplaces we feel satisfied leaving at the end of the day.

The evidence for well-being is there for both individuals and businesses. Regardless of your organization's current level of commitment, my purpose is to help YOU find healthy ways to shift to a more sustainable way of working. If you are reading this as an organizational leader, you may find approaches that enhance your culture, foster greater innovation, and ultimately deliver better results to your customers. And with even the smallest steps you can begin making your company work for you. By thriving together, we can go from working hell to working well.

CHAPTER 1

The state of well-being in the workplace

"If you want to go fast, go alone.
If you want to go far, go together."
—Proverb of disputed origin.

Before we dive into the strategies and tools, I want to share more about why I am writing this book. Like most people of a certain age, I have my own burnout story. When my first child was born, I came back from maternity leave into a new role at the same company. There were some organizational moves while I was gone, and the role I had coveted before I became a mom was offered to me. Yay, right?! While it was incredible to feel such support for my career development, it was a much bigger and highly visible role. And I had no juice to do it. I had a long commute and was not getting enough sleep, exercise, or anything else to keep my tank full. Eventually, I had to ask to move out of the high-status role and make peace with the hit to my growth trajectory. Now, you don't need to be a new parent to need a pivot. There can be any new stressor that sends you into burnout and survival mode. What we need and want from work can change all the time.

During the lockdown of the pandemic, we all were in survival mode. Literally. Even if we had our physical health, social isolation, constant change, collective trauma around racism, global conflict, and climate change impacted mental health for many. Add to the mix our always-on-work culture, dedicated to maintaining productivity, now extended beyond its normal boundaries into our kitchen or bedroom. Many of us turned into talking heads, sitting at a computer all day, going from video call to video call. Often without even the comfort of a smiling face, people reverted to being off video. I was one of the fortunate people to have a separate home office, and my husband would tell me that I would disappear for hours only to emerge for the family in a haze with a total lack of presence. I was becoming the robot that Corporate America wanted me to be, and worse, I had fully bought into operating that way.

While I'm not here to relive the pain of the pandemic and other widespread trauma, I do think there is a way to make work better. And we must try. Before I get to what that could look like, I want to clarify some key terms and research findings. This is an evolving landscape, but I will refer to these concepts and data points throughout the book.

Wellness vs. well-being

Wellness and well-being often get used interchangeably. For the sake of this book, my focus is more on well-being, but I will clarify the distinction I am making between the two. The Global Wellness Institute defines wellness[2] as "the active pursuit of activities, choices and lifestyles that lead to a state of holistic health." Both wellness and well-being tend to emphasize multiple dimensions, such as physical, mental, emotional, spiritual, and financial. WebMD Health Services describes[3] how well-being takes a more all-inclusive view of the various dimensions and how they "are intertwined and impact one another." Wellness tends to be about the individual choices we make. Alternatively, well-being is more collectively shaped.

Individual-focused wellness options alone may help people's stress management and overall capacity for a short while if they have time to take advantage. Companies who can afford to do so might offer access to wellness apps, yoga classes, or group meditation. Usually, they are connected to company benefits. Yet a recent large-scale study [4] of 46,000 UK workers found no evidence of actual workplace well-being gains from offering these options alone. Before you quit your favorite yoga class, it's important to note that there is a lot of other research supporting the value of yoga, meditation, and other stress-reduction techniques. But, when looking from a return on employer investment perspective, the research saw the most benefit from deeper organizational changes.

Dr. William Fleming, Research Fellow at the University of Oxford's Wellbeing Research Centre and author of the study, said[5], "There's growing consensus that organisations have to change the workplace and not just the worker." If we take into consideration the amount of time people spend at work, one can see how the workplace can have a disproportionate impact on our overall well-being. This is bigger than each individual's wellness choices. And there is a benefit to organizations that invest the time to make employee well-being a priority. Dr. Jan-Emmanuel De Neve, in his recent study[6] on Workplace Wellbeing and Firm Performance, demonstrated that well-being has a huge predictive impact on actual business outcomes, including better valuations, better profits, and better returns.

Starting by just understanding that well-being is an interconnected web of choices individuals, leaders and organizations make can help set us all up for success.

Burnout, stress, and workaholism

Some of the recent urgency around well-being stems from many people experiencing burnout in the workplace. In a recent Society for Human Resource Management (SHRM) survey on Employee Mental Health, they cited[7] that 44% of employees surveyed feel burned out at work. Other surveys have shown even higher numbers, especially when broken down by different demographics. But let's start by explaining what burnout is and how to know if you or others are impacted. First, the World Health Organization describes[8] burnout as "a syndrome conceptualized as resulting from chronic workplace stress that has not been successfully managed. It is characterized by three dimensions:

- feelings of energy depletion or exhaustion.
- increased mental distance from one's job, feelings of negativism or cynicism related to one's job, and
- reduced professional efficacy.

Burn-out refers specifically to phenomena in the occupational context and should not be applied to describe experiences in other areas of life." While burnout may be primarily experienced at work, we know from the well-being definition above that it still will co-mingle with the other dimensions of well-being. As such, work has a holistic impact on overall health and life satisfaction.

Unfortunately, the younger generations entering the workforce are already stressed out. A Gallup survey[9] found, "Compared with older generations today, the Gallup-WFF study said members of Gen Z are much more likely to report experiencing negative emotions such as stress, anxiety and loneliness." They are the newest members of our workforce, and we need them to want to stay in it so the rest of us can retire. Just kidding. (Sort of.) Ok, my Gen-X brethren, it's time to stop minimizing other generation's stress. It may be interpreted as whining or entitled, but history[10] has shown that older generations have been complaining about younger ones for thousands of years. Let it go. In their eBook[11] on Employee Fulfillment, Culture Partners share, "Millennials and Gen Z aren't the only ones who care about fulfillment; people of all ages and from all backgrounds want to find purpose and meaning in life, and in their work. And even if our work doesn't connect to our purpose in life, we can still find meaning in it." We all want to get the most out of our lives and work.

Yet the world is wildly different than even five years ago, let alone when some of us started work. Younger workers want to work differently and the stress and anxiety they already have upon even entering the workforce is limiting. LifeStance Health research[12] shows that "Gen Z struggles to maintain the same performance and productivity levels as their older counterparts due to their elevated stress and anxiety levels." Life stages make a difference, but millennials also are suffering. These are the generations shaping the future of work. If you aren't convinced from the heart, know that the American Institute for Stress has calculated[13] that "Job stress is estimated to cost the US industry more than $300 billion in losses due to absenteeism, diminished productivity, and accidents."

Chronic stress and burnout are just plain bad for business and our bodies. I remember watching a team member get wheeled out by paramedics due to stress-related heart palpitations. She had a great support network and an even better performance record. Yet a recent American Psychological Association Stress in America Survey[14] showed, "Around three in five adults (62%) said they don't talk about their stress overall because they don't want to burden others." Roughly the same number said that they think people just expect them to get over their stress. Warning: I'm about to reference the other "F-word" in business, FEELINGS. Other than having external counseling resources or being lucky enough to have a great people leader or teammates, many people don't have a lot of safe space for navigating feelings in the workplace.

Further exacerbating stress is the loneliness epidemic. US Surgeon General Vivek Murthy shared[15] the statistic, "One in two adults in America are living with measurable levels of loneliness, but the numbers are even higher among young people." While the data does show this is an issue, the wonderful thing is that work can be a place of connection for so many people. There does need to be an intentional focus on creating a quality work experience, though. A Harvard Business Review study[16] by Emma Seppälä and Marissa King showed that "Workplace engagement is associated with positive social relations that involve feeling valued, supported, respected, and secure. And the result of feeling socially connected, studies show, is greater psychological well-being, which translates into higher productivity and performance." It doesn't require a lot of time to create connection. Still, there are huge benefits to our stress levels, energy, and resilience if we can make it. SHRM's data[17] also shows that "workers who feel a strong sense of belonging at work are 2.5 times less likely to feel burned out." This statistic reinforces both our need for interconnectedness as a whole and how we all play a part in the broader system of workplace well-being.

Working long hours certainly can contribute to burnout by reducing time spent connecting with others or in activities that juice us. Workaholism is not just about working long hours; it's more about the internal compulsion to work to the detriment of other life activities. Just like alcohol or drugs, it can be a means to escape feelings or emotions we don't want to deal with. Because it is socially sanctioned, it can sometimes be hard to spot the difference between a disorder, burnout, and just struggling to manage work demands more healthily. Malissa Clark describes workaholism in her book, *Never Not Working: Why the Always-On Culture is Bad for Business—and How to Fix It.*[18] and as a Forbes contributor[19]. "There are a ton of external reasons someone may work long hours, or take on multiple jobs," she says. "Many times, it's financial—that income is necessary in order for their family to get by. Or maybe it's a demanding boss, or a busy time (e.g., tax season). Workaholism, in contrast, is driven by internal demands. It's that pit in our stomach nagging us when we're not working; a feeling that we 'ought to' or 'should be' working all the time...Sure, long hours are a part of workaholism, but it doesn't tell the whole story." It's important to differentiate between burnout and workaholism because different support well beyond this book may be needed on your journey towards greater well-being.

Connecting to business metrics

So why is well-being not a priority at all organizations? While I don't profess to know all the answers to that question, as it is certainly complex, there are clues. In general, most organizations use a variety of business metrics to monitor organizational health and performance. Recently, I heard a story about one CEO who was using email traffic as a proxy for measuring productivity. When they saw that email traffic was low on Fridays, they ordered everyone back into the office five days a week. While I don't know if that decision actually increased productivity or not, I am guessing that most people were using Friday to get their actual work done versus sending emails and sitting in meetings all day! Jen Fisher, a leader in Human Sustainability, writes[20], "The problem is productivity isn't a measure of outcome or quality. It's a measure of output—of busyness... But busy work doesn't always move the needle—not for the person doing it and not for the company they are doing it for. It can drive people to be busy at all costs, without evaluating if that busyness is creating any actual value." Now, many companies may be taking a more holistic approach but using some productivity metrics in isolation risks making decisions that create a culture ripe for burnout.

Another commonly used metric is engagement, which measures how good employees feel about their work involvement and their company. The Gallup organization has been tracking the connection between engagement and business performance for years. A recent analysis[21] by Gallup showed that companies with high engagement levels have lower turnover, less absenteeism, and better customer outcomes, resulting in a "a 23% difference in profitability." Gallup even found a connection between engagement and well-being; "when engagement and high well-being are both present, the impact on life evaluations is palpable. For these workers -- about 12% of the U.S. working population -- 92% are considered to be thriving." So, engagement surveys can be tools to support both well-being and profitability if a company uses them to create positive change.

Some companies may choose to measure business success via sustainable performance[22]. "Sustainable performance means coworkers do excellent work without falling into the traps of burnout or workaholism. Sustainable performance means your organization efficiently and effectively provides quality products and services, is blessed with low absenteeism and low staff turnover. All of this is good for the bottom line." If companies want to make employee well-being part of their strategy, the evidence is there that it is good for business. Whatever data leaders or colleagues need, any of the previous metrics or data points may help you get their buy-in to the well-being movement.

Closing

There is a well-being ceiling. The invisible barriers can be hard to spot. It's the co-worker who sends emails at 11 pm. It's the manager who tells you they worked all weekend in the office. But "don't worry, I don't expect that of you." It's the VP who declares, "I don't have time for a vacation." It's the person in the elevator who responds to "How are you?" with "I'm just so busy." That's just the temperature of the water, another way to describe the cultural expectations in an organization. I haven't even brought up the many structures, systems, and work design issues that also keep us working in industrial-age conditions.

Feeling seen and heard while being given the autonomy and flexibility to be our best selves doesn't have to be a pipe dream. Work doesn't have to be just about "acting your wage." Going into the office five days a week also isn't the one-stop solution to get back to normal that many CEOs think it is. There is no going "back." We need to look forward and determine what kind of work environment will sustain us holistically as human beings. Let AI appropriately be the robot.

Why am I telling you all of this? Perhaps you thought this book was just about what you can do to make work better for yourself. It is. But in these times of employee activism[23] on the rise, I want you to know that you can also "be the change." Burnout is contagious[24]. Wherever you sit in an organization, you always have a choice and a voice. We are all more powerful than we know. Then when we come together with our voices, we can really create healthier workplaces. The more of us who practice this, the more we'll be able to make collective shifts in how work gets done, how companies treat us, and how we treat each other. We don't need to wait. Throughout this book I will give you ideas for how you can think or act differently for yourself, but also how your own changes can create a ripple effect for others as well. I invite you to be part of the growing well-being movement by starting with yourself and sharing your learning with others.

CHAPTER 2

Working mindfully

"Many of us have a mind that measures self-worth in terms of productivity... We give ourselves no credit for just being present. And yet, if you asked the people you care about what they would like most from you, their answer is likely to be some version of 'your presence.'"
—Jan Chozen Bays.

There is no magic well-being formula for every person or every company. And every employee at the same company may have wildly different experiences. You're likely reading this book, though, because you are looking for some kind of transformation for yourself or others. To make change, what I've found to be the common thread is time and space to observe your thoughts, behaviors, and practices. After decades of working full-time in Corporate America, I had the support and privilege to transition to a part-time schedule for almost two years. By creating enough space to observe how I was working, I noticed the workaholic tendencies that ultimately fed an adrenaline junkie. Over time, I found my way back to more soul-nourishing practices. But you don't need to work part-time to get these benefits. Even my coaching clients who worked full-time hours also had better energy and productivity when they adopted more mindful ways of working.

Finding work-life harmony

Simply put, work-life harmony is a healthy and empowered way of approaching work, acknowledging that it is just one part of your life and not your life in totality. Like a symphony orchestra engages the strings, the brass, and the percussion to make music, there is a coming together to create a beautiful whole. The parts may not always be equal, but you know how to mindfully flow through your days, finding a pleasing arrangement. You are able to avoid burnout because you are working at a tempo that fits your life and needs. Work can be a source of satisfaction and meaning, but not to the consistent detriment of other parts of your life. This is the place on the spectrum between working ourselves sick and being sick of working. Work-life harmony is about saying yes to your whole self and seeing work as a part of who you are some of the time.

Bringing your whole self to work

The Bring Your Whole Self to Work movement, in spirit, was an attempt to honor that. Mike Robbins, in his book[25] on the topic, said, "Bringing our whole selves to work means showing up authentically, leading with humility, and remembering that we're all vulnerable, imperfect human beings doing the best we can." This is a beautiful human definition that creates space for learning, growth, and acceptance. One of the silver linings of the pandemic was seeing other non-perfected parts of people's lives—barking dogs, loud children, wilting plants, etc. I still laugh when I think of the Zoom call with a normally serious executive whose 7-year-old daughter was doing cartwheels behind him during the entire call. While he didn't skip a beat, I definitely felt more connected to the human across the screen.

In my experience working with teams, when people know and see each other as full human beings, greater trust can form, typically resulting in better outcomes. I saw a beautiful social media post where someone requested a mental health day, and within 20 minutes of clocking in, all her cases were reassigned. The response from her team was, "We got you." Now, her whole team also knows that it is safe to make the request and that others will be in support when they need it, too.

However, for employees to feel safe enough to bring their whole selves to work, a degree of psychological safety is needed. Dr. Amy Edmondson, a Harvard professor, defines[26] psychological safety as "The belief that one will not be punished or humiliated for speaking up with ideas, questions, concerns or mistakes." So, in environments with low psychological safety, it can be very hard for people to share their concerns, especially about personal needs. For example, let's say that your sister is performing in a one-night-only show, and you'd like to leave work early to attend. Of course, as a responsible employee, you plan to tend to the tasks that need to be completed in a timely manner. But if you don't have the psychological safety to be honest with your manager, you may feel like you need to lie to get your needs met. Most of us feel conflicted about even little lies, and it can create a precarious challenge in any relationship.

Organizations can help employees and their managers bring their whole selves to work with fair and consistent decision-making through clear company policies and program guidelines. When one of my former employers launched flexible work arrangements, employees were not asked to explain why they wanted to work differently to avoid possible judgment and bias in the approval process. Rather, they were asked just how they planned to accommodate the work in the new arrangement and how it would benefit them and the company. So, it didn't matter if you needed time to take care of an aging parent or wanted to take mornings to surf; flexibility was there to support the various parts of yourself.

There is no doubt that we all have our own level of comfort when it comes to bringing our whole selves to work. Some of the discomfort is environmental, and some is personal. To support greater well-being in the workplace, we all need to test our assumptions and be brave. And that is hard, especially in fast-moving, high-performance cultures. But first, we need to create enough mental space to articulate what we need and be transparent about the requests we have for others. We may not always get what we want, but we can open the door to more conversation and connection, thereby creating more choices.

Embracing mindfulness

Mastering work-life harmony also means we practice being mindful. Jon Kabat-Zinn, in his book[27] *Mindfulness for Beginners*, says, "Mindfulness reminds us that it is possible to shift from a doing mode to a being mode through the application of attention and awareness." I know a lot of people may struggle with this, as I often do. But for the sake of this book and approach, all you need to practice is just enough mindfulness to pause when needed. I will share ways to go even deeper, but just a few key mindfulness concepts can help tremendously. I've broken them into the different intelligence centers (mind, heart, body) so that you may see where you already have traction or where there is more opportunity to explore.

Mind:

Mindfulness may start with noticing, which allows you to create an observer level of awareness of what's going on for you in a given moment. That might be your thoughts, emotions, or bodily sensations. The idea behind noticing is to create some balance between the stories we may be telling ourselves and what may be really happening. For example, imagine you are presenting a new initiative to some senior-level executives. On one level, you are likely to share some prepared content. But then you get a question, and you start sweating. Then your mind tells you that you must not be doing a good job if they had that question. The next question has you thinking they don't like your proposal and you should just leave the room. As an outside observer, one may only see the facts of a sweaty presenter sharing slides and some people asking a few questions. But connecting with your internal observer to acknowledge that you are creating some stories in your own mind can often bring you back into balance. Then, you can be in the right headspace for meaningful discussion and intentionally choose how you'd like to show up.

Many of you may have heard of the concept of being present. While there is no exact definition, the concept I like is one where we can be fully engaged in the current moment without distraction or the noise of internal dialogue. This may be hard, but the good news is that it can be practiced. We can also give ourselves a lot of grace in being present by just noticing when we have slipped away and bringing ourselves back to the moment at hand. The ability to return to presence can help us be more resilient and more in tune with ourselves, also alleviating stress and anxiety as the stories we tell ourselves fade more into the background.

Heart:

Thoughts can also bring about emotions. Dr. Susan David, in her book[28] *Emotional Agility*, describes emotions as "signposts that indicate what's important to us." When we can peel back the layers of what data the emotions are giving us, we can begin to understand what value, for example, is coming up in the moment so we can take action to feel more aligned. One of my coaching clients had a very strong value of humility, and when meetings shifted to virtual during the pandemic, he found himself very uncomfortable watching himself on video. Yet he acknowledged that some people may interpret off-camera status as being disengaged, and that was creating some healthy tension for him. We figured out how to hide his self-view on video calls, and he found he was much more comfortable being himself and showing up as engaged as he felt.

Being mindful of our emotions also means that we don't allow only certain emotions to be experienced. For example, I'm generally a happy, energetic personality. But several years ago, I realized that my strength of positivity was also creating suffering by not honoring the more uncomfortable emotions that made me whole. And by staying in denial and not acknowledging hurt or fear, I couldn't try to make my situation better. Rather, I filled myself up with distractions like binge-worthy dramas to take my mind off the pain. Work also filled some of the holes in the hurt I was experiencing, which partially contributed to my workaholic ways. Many of us don't have a huge emotional vocabulary—sad, mad, and happy may be the most of it for some of us and that's ok. By becoming more emotionally intelligent, we can create new awareness to possibly reduce stress, improve relationships and gain more job satisfaction.

Challenging emotions may also emerge when we have negative self-talk. Most of us have a judge in our head that is frequently telling us all the bad things that we do or how we "should" have done something differently. Imposter syndrome is a common example of that noisy judge telling us we're not worthy or not good enough, only to be found a fraud someday. Noticing the thought can also help us create enough space for curiosity to find a new way to respond. Is this a fact or a feeling? Our emotional state often follows these thoughts and if we can clear the irrational thoughts and fears, we can better maintain our emotional equilibrium.

While mindfulness may not stop the inner critic from chiming in, we can respond in a kind, less judgmental way. What would we say to a friend? Sometimes just asking ourselves that very question can put us on alert that we are judging ourselves too harshly. In my first year of business school, I was really challenged by so much change, school stress, and adapting to a new environment. I would notice that even finding out someone completed their homework before me could send me into a catastrophic spin. Instead of going down the path of feeling anxious and telling myself that I was behind, I took a kinder approach by changing the self-talk to "everyone goes at their own pace." By adopting a more self-compassionate approach, I was able to regulate my stress levels and even lean into my strengths to feel more empowered about my experience.

Body:

One of the simplest ways to create mindfulness and reduce stress is to start with your breath. Breathing as a tool is somewhat ironic because it's automatic; we don't really think about it. But our breath is connected to our parasympathetic nervous system, which can help us control our stress levels and the fight, flight, and freeze responses we may have in a situation. Just breathing in for 4 seconds and then out for 6 seconds can help settle our body so we can be more present with what is happening to us. Try that now, please. (What's 10 seconds in your day?)

For those of us desk jockeys who may not get much movement in our days, we may feel very disconnected from our bodies in general. Yet our bodies often know what is going on way before our minds do. Mapping sensations to patterns of thoughts or feelings can be a helpful shortcut to self-awareness. For example, you may feel tension in your throat area when you want to speak up and you're afraid your idea will be judged. Or you may feel a hot, tingly, burning sensation in your stomach when someone makes you angry.

Especially when we are triggered, our bodies go into autopilot and can support our being more impulsive in our reactions. An impulsive response to someone interrupting you could be talking louder or shutting down. I'd guess that either one could get in the way of having a productive conversation with a colleague. Whatever our triggers and physiological responses are, by paying attention to our bodies, we can create that little bit of space for more choice in our response. That may be as simple as taking a breath to notice you feel shut down and connecting back to what action you need to take to get the meeting back on track.

The last thing to capture in the body section is body shape, which is the form we hold our body in, often reflective of our emotional state. Take a few seconds now, and just notice your posture. Now, hunch your shoulders, hang your neck to your chest, and say to yourself, "Today will be a great day!" Next, put your shoulders back and hold your head up high, making yourself feel as regal as possible, and say to yourself again, "Today will be a great day!" Which body shape did you believe more?

I remember watching my son play baseball years ago and knowing from so many yards away how he was feeling about his game that day. He was playing shortstop and started off the game head up high and ready to play. Then he missed a ball and I noticed his shoulders were a little hunched over for the next couple of innings. For the third inning, he started as a pitcher, and as more and more batters got hits off him, I could barely see his face; his head was hanging so low. When he went back to shortstop, he looked hunched up and miserable. Needless to say, he didn't have his best game in the field or at bat. Whatever negative thoughts he had coursing through his mind were showing up in his body and sabotaging his play that day.

Paying attention to your body shape can be another avenue to foster awareness of your mood or mental state. Once you have that recognition, you can then figure out the thoughts you need to possibly course-correct, emotions to honor, or new shapes to explore. As we continue our journey together, I will pull through some of these concepts into the actions you can take to support you along the way.

Exploring purpose

Staying mindful of our values and needs can help light the path to our sense of purpose. For the sake of this book, when I use the word purpose, I mean purpose with a little "p." There is much talk in the business world about finding one's Purpose, big "P," which is bigger and weightier and more like a life calling. When I think of purpose, it's a little lighter and more connected to what I want to get from an experience. So, in that fashion we can have a lot of purpose throughout all facets of our life. What do I want to get out of writing this book? What growth do I want to get out of working for this company or in this role? What experience do I want to get out of signing up to be in a musical with my daughter? Whatever IT is, taking even a few minutes to get clear on your intention can transform your experience and your attitude toward whatever happens or doesn't happen.

One of the tools that supported my business school experience was being clear on my purpose in going and what I wanted to get out of it. Early on, I created a laundry list of desired outcomes and whenever I would get stressed, I would go back to that list. For example, there were always corporate presentations to attend, and there would be a buzz on campus as to who was attending what. My fear of missing out (FOMO) would kick in, and I'd try to figure out how I was going to fit it all into my busy schedule. Then, I would go back to my list and realize that I could let both the anxiety and the activity go. It wasn't part of my business school purpose.

Many people take jobs because they are inspired by an organization's purpose. In recent decades, a lot of companies have created amazing vision and mission statements that have attracted and connected us to them. For some lucky ones, work is where you are self-actualized and really living your true, big "P" Purpose in life. And hopefully others are working at a place that still allows you to take advantage of your gifts and strengths and feel tremendous job satisfaction. This connection to purpose makes work meaningful, but it also may be why you are reading this book right now. You may be so connected to the company's purpose that it is hard to set boundaries or create a more sustainable flow between life and work.

One of my coaching clients felt deeply connected to her company's purpose. So much so that when I asked her what would enable her to dial back her work a little to make space for other life needs, her answer shocked me. "Honestly, I think I would need to get too sick to work." Alarm bells started going off in my head that some of us would sacrifice our own lives to serve the needs of our company and customers. No matter how noble the mission is, I don't think many leadership teams would want their employees to harm themselves in the process of delivering it. But it also takes a special leadership team to create enough psychological safety to make sure that doesn't happen.

Closing

Well-being isn't just about cutting back your hours and taking yoga classes. It means that you can be fully present and as dedicated and productive as the situation warrants. But you can still separate enough from work to step back into your other identities and see work as part of your life. When you're there, you're fully there. And when you're not at work, you are also present in relationships, hobbies, sports, volunteering or whatever activities make you whole.

Now, nothing I have shared here is new information. But the key point to this book is knowing that you have choices. And the first step is to acknowledge the space of choice. In a culture where we wear BUSY as a badge of honor, we are so caught up in the motion of moving from one thing to the next that we may forget to create space. Mastering work-life harmony starts with having enough mindfulness to stay true to your whole self and whatever purpose(s) give you meaning. And hopefully having a lot of purpose also creates the motivation to start taking even the smallest of steps in your desired direction.

Chapter highlights:

- Work-life harmony is a healthy and empowered way of approaching work, acknowledging that it is just one part of your life and not your life in totality. You are able to flow with the various needs in your life, in and out of work.

- Bringing your whole self to work is about showing up authentically and recognizing we are all vulnerable and imperfect humans. We all play a role in making it psychologically safe to be our whole selves and greater trust can form when we can.

- We can embrace mindfulness from any of the intelligence centers: mind, heart, and body. This can entail noticing the stories we tell ourselves and being present. We can also access our heart space by tending to our emotions and ensuring compassionate self-talk. Using our breath and noticing our body shape and our sensation patterns are other ways to create more choice in how we show up in our day to day.

- By tapping into small "p" purpose, we can imbue more meaning and connection in our various work and life activities. This also helps us to be more intentional with our time and reframe disappointments.

And...ACTION! Simple tools and practices to play with:

1. A simple way to tap into the change you want to see in your work-life harmony is to create a From...To vision statement. It can be as long or short as you want. Some examples:

   a. From scattered to grounded.

   b. From guilt-ridden long days to time focused on the people who care about me.

   c. From overwhelmed to overwhelmed with joy.

2. In the deadtime, before a meeting officially starts, ask easy questions to get to know your colleagues on a deeper level. Before you groan, you can make these as benign or edgy as you want. "What is your first memory of trust?" "What color(s) remind you of home?" "What food could you not be paid to eat?" For a list of icebreaker questions, go to my website, www.workinghelltoworkingwell.com.

3. When we can catch ourselves in our stories, it can also be helpful to create an explicit pause. You can do that by noticing that you need to take a breath before responding to a question, for example. While three seconds feel like an eternity in our brain, it likely just feels like a short pause to others. If you need a slightly longer pause in conversation, you can also create a planned catchphrase. For example, "I need a second to process your question" or "I really appreciate this conversation." That can give your mind the time needed to respond effectively.

4. Emotion wheels[29] can be incredibly helpful in deepening our understanding of ourselves. You can use it to distinguish whether a feeling of surprise stems from awe or confusion, for instance. Try this daily reflection on your emotions:

   a. What was my strongest feeling today at work? What triggered it?

   b. What emotion did I feel most comfortable with? What did I learn from it?

    c.   What emotion did I move away from? What does this tell me?

    d.   What action(s) will I take from what I observed in this exercise?

5.   One quick practice to ground yourself is to just find your feet. Go ahead and give it a try. Notice how they feel on the floor. Do they need a stretch or a flex? What happens when you push them into the ground a little bit? Do you notice any response elsewhere in your body when you do? This can take literally one second and be imperceptible to anyone around you, but it can help bring you back to a present, centered self.

6.   Have a little fun playing with little "p" purpose. Think of a daily or weekly activity, and the more mundane, the better. How can you create more intent and meaning in it? For example, instead of just thinking, "I'm commuting," reframe it to "This is my time to separate work and life so I can be more present in both." Try this exercise with any activity, at or out of work, and notice if anything shifts for you.

CHAPTER 3

Creating time and space for more choice

"Lack of direction, not lack of time, is the problem. We all have 24-hour days."
—Zig Ziglar.

This chapter is designed to help you start creating some time and/or space. While clock time has a physical/metaphysical construct of seconds, hours, days, and years, how we actually experience the sensation of time is going to vary wildly by person and culture. For kicks, set a one-minute timer and just sit in a comfortable position and close your eyes. Yes...try it now, 'cause you're here, and what's one minute really?

Ok, you can come back now. What came up for you? Some things you might have noticed:

- Mind:
  o Lots of to-do's
  o Wondering why you're doing this...
  o Focus
  o Your add_____
- Heart
  o Frustrated
  o Open
  o Judgmental

- o   Your add_____
- Body
  - o   Hard to sit still/fidgety
  - o   Relaxed, body at ease
  - o   Breathing cadence
  - o   Your add_____

Our relationship with time is unique to ourselves. We all see it and think of how to use it differently, and culture plays a big role. That culture may be your organizational, regional, or ethnic culture, just to name a few. But what you noticed in that 1-minute exercise might give you a sense of how you orient yourself to time. If you found yourself stuck in your to-do list feeling fidgety, you might have more of a task orientation. Or if you just stayed very present in the moment, you might have more comfort with downtime, the space between different tasks, or just rest itself. There are a lot of different time constructs, and you don't need to know them all technically, but the most important thing is to notice for yourself how you think about time.

And sometimes, it's helpful to have a discussion with your partners about how they view time. You may leave this chapter with some conversations you'd like to have with your manager, significant other, or teammates. To give you an example of what that may look like, I'll share that my husband and I have very different relationships with time. Going to the airport is a source of stress for many people, and once we had kids, this task ruffled some feathers in our relationship. Before one flight, I asked my husband, "What time do you want to leave for the airport?" and he said 8 am. So, I was ready to go at 8 am with bags by the door. But that still left us squabbling and rushing around, getting kids' shoes on and the like for several minutes before catching our ride.

The next time we went to the airport, I asked a better question, "So if you want to leave at 8 am, what time do you want me to be ready?" The new answer was 7:45 am, so we had time to connect on any last-minute needs. In that experience, I noticed that 1) I had a more fluid approach to time, e.g., 8ish is fine for me, and 2) my conditions of satisfaction for being ready were not the same as his, e.g., ready means everything is done, not just bags by the door. In the workplace, I have heard many spats over the term "end of day (EOD) or end of business (EOB)." For some, that means 5 pm, and for others, that means midnight! The important insight through both these stories is the importance of clarifying expectations and desired outcomes.

Once we make our implicit expectations explicit, we create some space for negotiation, e.g., 7:45 am vs. 8 am. This is critical for being able to meet our needs, as well as those of others. First, we need to look at a few common stories we may tell ourselves that can sabotage our best intentions of having more time or space for the things we want. The easy way to remember this approach is "More Time Now."

Story 1: "More is better."

More is always better, right? More money. More clients. More ice cream. As a leadership coach, I have been fortunate to have worked with a lot of highly accomplished clients, yet I have noticed that, for many, a fear of inadequacy still plagues them. Sometimes, that looks like a desire for extrinsic validation of their worth through promotions, compensation, or high-profile responsibilities. While these aspirations are natural, I've observed—and experienced myself—that external validation only provides temporary satisfaction before the need for the next "hit" sets in. This constant drive often makes it difficult to pause and appreciate what we already have, leaving an undercurrent of discontent.

This pursuit of more often manifests as overperforming behaviors. For example, I met with countless employees who just wanted to get promoted and be seen for all their hard work. Many employees would take on large projects with limited resources, working late into the evenings in hopes of standing out. Performance systems that reward "above and beyond" efforts often reinforce these behaviors. While excellence and high-quality work require time, overperforming often comes at the expense of personal well-being.

This mindset can also be a challenging behavior for leaders of teams. For example, one of my clients oversaw a large internal operations team, and he wanted to make sure they had the brand of being excellent service providers. As admirable as that is, there was also an expectation for everything to be of the highest standard, without the necessary resources to achieve it consistently. My client repeatedly told me with high hopes that everything would be great once he had more resources. While there is no doubt some truth in that, I did challenge him by asking, "What would you do differently if this was really all the resources you had?" When we have this amazing vision of excellence, it can be hard to let go of it and face the reality of the situation. However, holding on too tightly can trap us and our teams in a cycle of unrealistic expectations where, ultimately, no one wins.

Addressing concerns about expectations can require significant courage, especially in organizations where it doesn't feel safe to highlight the imbalance between demands and resources. We can still be excellent, just maybe not at everything or all the time. One of my favorite managers excelled at re-aligning outcomes with the resources available, and the entire team benefited from his skillful negotiations with stakeholders. Often, in playing out our own fears in our judging mind, we forget that people can be quite reasonable.

Other clients have also seen this fear of inadequacy translate to behaviors that look like overpreparing. One client struggled with her manager's challenging communication style. When presenting to him, he often picked at her thinking and background data. So, her response was to spend a lot of time preparing for all the possible questions he might ask her. While there is nothing wrong with being primed, it does make me question how much that preparation is driven by our sense of self-worth rather than a focus on solving the problem at hand. What is the work needed to keep things moving forward and can I plan to just that level? Things change so much in our VUCA (volatility, uncertainty, complexity, ambiguity) world[30]; preparing just enough leaves us flexibility and energy for collaboration and co-creation. Now I realize there are enough evil bosses out there to make our lives miserable, but a lot of what we think they can do to hurt our job status or well-being may just be in our imagination. We end up causing ourselves more harm than they do by overworking to meet possibly false expectations. So, it can be worthwhile to validate our assumptions. If your boss is markedly unrealistic, you may need to find new avenues for support instead.

Interestingly, I see senior executives get caught off guard by this "more is better" mindset as well. They may reach out to someone requesting a report or some information. Then, they receive back a 150-page PowerPoint deck that a person or team pulled an all-nighter to create. "But now the executive knows how hard I work and how much I know! And more information is better, right?!" Maybe sometimes but building capability in delivering "just enough" is likely more helpful for your stakeholders and whoever is charged with doing the work. However, I do acknowledge that it can be hard to have enough information or time with executives to know exactly what problem they are trying to solve or what decision to make. There is no easy answer, but it can be helpful to just pause throughout your day to ask yourself, "Is this just enough?"

If you see yourself getting caught in overperforming or overpreparing, you may want to stay aware of what fear is playing out. What is the little judge in your head saying to you? How can you be more kind to yourself? These fears feel real and are painful. And some fears may be realized, but test some of the practices out and see if any can give you a little more time or less stress in your workday.

Story 2: "I don't have enough time."

This is the one expression that I hear endlessly and which does require some unpacking. Reality check—there will always only be 24 hours in a day. You will never have enough time for everything you want to or feel like you should do. Now that I have stressed and depressed you, let's move to the good news. Everyone has this same exact problem. Yep, even Beyoncé has only 24 hours in a day. But if we look at this just from an actual hour in a day perspective, we will only be addressing part of the problem. So, the first question we need to ask ourselves is, "Time for what?".

One challenge embedded into the "I don't have enough time" story is a fear of failure. And that fear may manifest in different ways. For example, it may look like failure in the form of not being at a certain standard. I see some people leaders get hooked into spending a lot of time micromanaging their team in very specific ways that they would like work done. Trust and competence are certainly important factors, but reassessing your standards and redefining what satisfactory completion looks like can help free up time for other priorities at work or in life. As individuals performing the work, it's also helpful to check with your stakeholders and yourself as to what the conditions of success are. There is always more that can be done, but will that extra hour, day, or week contribute to a 1% difference, and is that a meaningful return on investment?

Some people leaders get into the weeds with employees as a matter of integrity. "I wouldn't ask them to do something I wouldn't do myself." That is very honorable, but it also may be a coded way of saying I need to be "in" the work to make sure it gets done to a certain standard. Employees no doubt appreciate that a leader understands the challenges they face and has a realistic view of what it takes to complete a task. But jumping in with them can also impact their feelings of autonomy and growth. The choice is always yours, but rolling up your sleeves to work alongside them often comes with a time cost that is worth examining.

Redefining success and failure can also apply to your personal habits. If I commit to meditating and doing yoga five days a week, how do I get clear on my conditions of success? Can I let go of the perfect 20-minute meditation and 40-minute home yoga session? That is dreamy but not going to happen every day, and I don't need to beat myself up over it. For example, what if I reframed to, what do I have time for today? Today, I have time for a 3-minute meditation and a 12-minute yoga video if I can wake up 15 minutes early. Or maybe I need to ask my husband to help by taking my daughter to school so I get that extra 15 minutes in my day. No matter the approach, I have honored my commitment and consistency, and that is enough. You can always check back in with your purpose to help you redefine success to mitigate the fear of failure.

Another stress-inducing dynamic is thinking we are a failure if we need to ask for help. Generally, most American organizations have practices that reward individual achievement based on the principles of meritocracy. Many of us have internalized the belief that success requires being a lone superhero or figuring out everything on our own. This may be possible and learning new things is a source of self-efficacy, but it also can be a time trap.

When I run CliftonStrengths[31] assessment sessions for teams, participants get a list of their top 34 strengths in order. A key message in the workshop is that when we play to our strengths, we are bringing our own unique contributions to work. Yet, the first thing I often notice is people focusing on their weaker areas, lamenting that they don't excel in those strengths. Other than completely missing the purpose of the assessment, it is a prime example of time getting wasted, thinking we need to do it all to be successful. The beauty of doing this exercise in a team setting is uncovering others who possess the strengths you lack, allowing you to lean on them. Recognizing how black-and-white thinking about success contributes to stress and self-judgment can help alleviate the feeling of having no time.

Story 3: "Must do it now."

In our always-on work cultures, it is very easy to be in a reactive mode all day. There is often a high sense of urgency, not always balanced with one of importance or prioritization. But what makes something urgent? Deadlines contribute, of course, but usually, a task is urgent because we need to do something for somebody else. And we don't want to disappoint because of our own fear of rejection.

This fear has also spawned a default mode of being highly responsive all the time. Personally and professionally, most of us are addicted to getting those three little dots and just waiting for the response. A couple of years ago, one of my clients told me that the hour before we spoke he was in a live meeting with some people, simultaneously emailing other people while also replying to screen chats and texts from another set of people on his phone. Our brains were just not built for that level of information switching. It's no wonder so many of us feel chronically distracted and experience a crisis of presence. But what would happen if we didn't respond right away?

Unfortunately, according to Dr. Malissa Clark[32], "the pandemic has exacerbated what scholars have called the cycle of responsiveness—a phenomenon where we become used to that immediate response to a work email, so we expect immediate responses from our coworkers, and we also feel pressured to respond quickly ourselves." I've always found it interesting when I receive requests with no specified timelines, as if an immediate answer is simply assumed. Often, we reinforce this expectation by responding right away, even when a prompt reply might not actually be necessary. It takes a lot of discipline to stay focused on what we need to do when there are so many ways to be disrupted. This is where taking that mindful pause can help interrupt the fear of rejection taking over from your productive intentions. You can pay it forward, too, by embedding your timelines into your own requests of others so they don't feel the need to reply right away.

A close cousin of responsiveness is overcommitting, usually a result of not feeling comfortable saying no. And we all want to be helpful or work on those really important projects, right? Yet by saying yes to so many things, we often lose sight of what is being sacrificed, which is often sleep, exercise, and time with family and friends. I have fallen victim to overcommitting more times than I'd like to admit, and my well-being has taken a hit, as expected. Ironically, it was usually my own tendencies causing the problem. In the spirit of being helpful, I would offer to take on work that no one asked me to do. So, I created a mantra for myself, "Just because I can, doesn't mean I should." It's a privilege to have gifts to share with others, but we must remember there are only 24 hours in a day. The good news is that we can practice saying no in safe, low-stakes situations to strengthen that skill and stay aligned with our greater purpose. We can also support each other by celebrating when someone sets boundaries and respecting their decision.

Meetings are another area where we often find ourselves overcommitted. FOMO is a common reason people feel they can't skip a meeting, but it's also tied to a fear of rejection. We may tell ourselves that missing a meeting means losing out on jokes or discussions and being excluded from the "in-group." While that might happen, mindfully weighing the tradeoffs and making an intentional decision can help you feel more at peace with the outcome. An interesting twist to this pattern is that some people won't decline meetings for fear of triggering other people's fear of rejection! But it is still worth examining your calendar.

One busy executive I know canceled all her standing internal meetings and asked people to re-schedule with various other leaders on her team. To be more purposeful with her time, she set a guideline for what kinds of meetings would make sense to include her in. By communicating her intention and approach, her team members didn't take her meeting cancellations personally. Whatever process you choose, slowing down to be more intentional can help break the cycle of always-on, hustle-driven work habits. By recognizing these behaviors in others, we can act as a mirror, encouraging them to take their time, say no, and decline meetings without fearing rejection.

Closing

Taking a moment to step out of reactive mode and become more mindful allows us to observe what's happening in the moment. What stories are we telling ourselves? What patterns or default responses are shaping our actions? When we feel time-poor, it's counterintuitive to imagine that slowing down could help, but without pausing to "read the signs," we risk heading in the wrong direction or burning out before we reach our destination.

Fear, in any form, triggers similar physical responses in our body, often putting us into fight, flight, or freeze mode. Daniel Goleman, author of *Emotional Intelligence*[33], describes this as an "amygdala hijack[34]," where the amygdala overrides our frontal lobes, shutting down rational thought and heightening emotional responses. While the adrenaline rush may make us feel temporarily alert, the continuous release of cortisol and other stress hormones can wreak havoc on our health, contributing to all kinds of health problems, such as[35] weight gain, heart disease, headaches, depression, and sleep problems. If that thought stresses you out, take heart: even just 10 minutes a day[36] of key activities can bring stress down.

To channel our energy effectively, we need to understand the triggers driving our behavior at work. Recognizing our fears helps us regain a sense of control and autonomy while also shedding light on how our habits influence the broader work environment. For example, a star employee sending emails at midnight may unintentionally signal that late-night work is the path to recognition. A manager joining meetings on vacation might set unrealistic expectations for availability. Pausing to acknowledge these fears and habits in a mindful, safe way helps calm our nervous systems and opens the door to healthier, more productive alternatives.

Chapter highlights:

- This chapter explored our relationship with time, highlighting fear-based behaviors that limit our sense of having the time and space for greater choice.
- The first fear is the fear of inadequacy. I captured this with "More is better" thinking. This fear often plays out in overperforming and overpreparing behaviors that suck our time and energy.
- The second common fear is a fear of failure. The refrain "I don't have enough time" rings loudly with this fear. Often, we see a drive to a certain standard and an aversion to asking for help getting in the way of more efficient and effective behaviors.
- Lastly, the fear of rejection is another common one. There is a compulsion that we "Must do it now" to please people. This may express itself as hyper-responsiveness and overcommitting, limiting our ability to work mindfully.

And...ACTION! Simple tools and practices to play with:

1. Time for what? Create a mini-purpose or why statement to motivate you to find more time. One avenue is to just complete this sentence stem: If I had more time, it would nourish me to.... (Examples: Play catch with my daughter, read a book, take a walk with my partner, garden, etc.).

2. Look at conditions of success or your standards. Set a timer on a task. When the timer goes off, ask yourself if this is just enough. Or seek out the requester to confirm it meets their conditions of success before doing additional work. If someone is asking this of you, consider whether it is at least a 20% gain to go back and keep refining.

3. Ask for help once a day. It can be as easy as asking someone to get something off the high shelf or carry in the groceries. As your comfort grows, ask for help with bigger ticket items that feel more vulnerable.

4. Put a due date in email requests so people can negotiate or feel like they don't need to respond immediately.

5. Practice saying no. Again, start with the easy stuff if this is hard. And if you don't believe "No." is a complete sentence, find your catchphrase that resonates. For example, "I'd love to help, but can't for the foreseeable future." If you'd rather practice a "Whole Body Yes," check out the Conscious Leadership Group's guide[37].

Support others in their practice by applauding them when they say no.

6. Create a Mantra for yourself. A mantra is just a word or phrase you can repeat to yourself when you need it or during meditation. Some examples:

   a. I am enough

   b. I am calm

   c. Just because I can doesn't mean I should (my personal one!)

CHAPTER 4

How can I be truer to myself at work?

"Don't ask what the world needs. Ask what
makes you come alive and go do it. Because what
the world needs is people who have come alive."
—Howard Thurman.

Now that you have looked at the fears that may have hijacked some of your best intentions, hopefully you've created some space to meaningfully design your work experience. The greatest benefit of a mindful approach to work is the clarity it brings, allowing you to align your intentions with your attention.

Needs: What do I really need from work?

Most of us must work so we can live in modern society. Basic physiological needs are real, and that may be your focus, and I don't want to minimize that. But I do think we can find a healthier balance and make work better than just a means to survival. That could simply be operating less from our reptilian brain's fear center or finding more time for things that energize us and bring us joy. One way to do this is to get more in touch with the needs that motivate our behavior. The Cambridge Dictionary defines needs as "the things you must have for a satisfactory life." While a promotion may seem like a need in itself, it often represents a deeper desire we're trying to fulfill, with the promotion serving as a tangible, externally valued expression of that need.

The earliest well-known needs framework is Abraham Maslow's Hierarchy of Needs[38]. In 1943, Abraham Maslow introduced his theory whereby people are motivated by the following need areas: physiological, safety and security, love and belonging, esteem and self-actualization. Sounds pretty aligned with many well-being dimensions, eh?

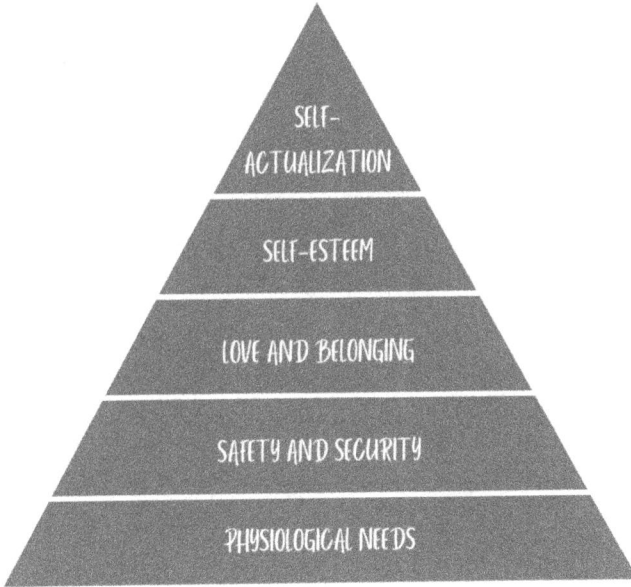

Other frameworks include David Rock's Neuroleadership Institute's SCARF model[39] and Marshall Rosenberg's Non-Violent Communication Needs and Emotions model[40]. Yet in all of them it is clear that when there is pain or fear in a need not being met, there will likely be suffering. As Marshall Rosenberg said[41], "There are no positive or negative emotions, just emotions we feel when our needs are met and emotions we feel when our needs are not met." Emotions can signal an unmet need, so staying attuned to them can help us recognize the underlying need. There is much to be gained by understanding all these frameworks more deeply, but I'm giving you some shortcuts to start with because I know you're busy!

Do you know what you need from your work? Keep in mind that work isn't limited to your job—it includes anything requiring mental or physical effort to achieve a result. This could encompass volunteering, caregiving, education, hobbies, or anything else you invest in. Your "work" may shift in importance or commitment over time, so it's important to stay aware of these needs. There's likely a voice—big or small—urging you to pay attention. Regularly tuning into your body and emotions can help amplify that voice. The sooner you recognize your needs, the sooner you can address them and find greater satisfaction in new possibilities.

Below is a short list of common social-emotional needs:

Sense of purpose and meaning	Creativity
Autonomy and ability to self-direct work	Play and fun
Respect and emotional safety	Contribution to business and/or society
Recognition for accomplishments	Beauty and inspiration
Learning and intellectual stimulation	Community

One place to start identifying needs is by looking at times in your day when you feel more profound emotions, both highs and lows. They may be pointing to needs being met or not. For example, you may have felt shut down in a meeting, but the meaning of that experience could be due to different reasons:

- Perhaps you felt disappointed your idea didn't get the approval to move ahead which might point to an autonomy or accomplishment need.
- Or the way the meeting ran, you felt slighted regarding your expertise regardless of whether the project went through, which could point to a need for status or respect.
- Or your project did get approved but not with a team to work on it, which may have you feeling overwhelmed or alone in your efforts. That could point to a need for collaboration or broader contribution.

Whatever the emotions are, they give you the gift of clarity.

Several years ago, I took time off from corporate work when my husband's job took us to Australia for a family adventure. Despite the career gap, the experience helped me clarify what I truly missed and wanted from work. I uncovered what I call the Big 3 Drivers—my most important needs—represented by the three "I's": Impact, Intellectual Challenge, and adult Interaction (two years with infants and toddlers really highlighted that). Identifying these higher-order needs opens up different ways to fulfill them. While I couldn't work in Australia, I found other ways to meet these needs, like writing children's books (intellectual challenge) and starting a writer's group (adult interaction). It wasn't necessary to have all three needs fulfilled at once, but understanding what I required made me more creative in finding options to satisfy them.

Identity: Who am I?

Sometimes, our sense of identity can sabotage us as well. When I first began working with one of my coaching clients, she was very quiet in meetings, feeling she hadn't earned the right to contribute to broader business discussions because of her job title. Over our time together, she grew to trust herself more and stopped defining herself solely as "the Senior Manager." As she shared more of her brilliance and confidence, people started noticing. She was eventually invited to an important global meeting, and when we met afterward, she described feeling like Cinderella. After months of seeing herself as the lowly servant, she was able to step into the role of the exuberant belle of the ball.

Identity doesn't just have to be a role; it can also be shaped by how we think we need to show up at work. Whether intentional or not, I felt my work persona was that of the upbeat, positive cheerleader—always ready to say, "We can do this." While that's part of who I am, it became limiting when I resisted feeling anger in response to difficult situations. Not only can that breed resentment, but there is a lot of energy that gets bottled up and can't be used elsewhere. I had my own coach tell me to be curious about feelings of anger and see what would happen if I allowed myself to really feel it. Well, an opportunity presented itself with my husband, and while he likely didn't appreciate my experiment, wow, did I like angry Lindsay! She was sassy and powerful and stood up for her needs. Of course, angry Lindsay eventually went away, and we worked things out in an honest and respectful way. But I was left with the knowledge that I could let "bad" feelings in and I could handle them, acknowledging and tending to the needs showing up.

Just as discomfort can influence our behaviors, our strengths also shape how our identity is reflected in the choices we make. One of my very technical clients often struggled with her role as a people leader. She was incredibly strong technically and was a great coach for her team. However, that subject matter expert pull sometimes made it hard for her to step away and let some team members make mistakes and learn in their own way. So, she often felt the tensions between two identities, the incredibly strong subject matter expert and the still-learning people leader. It's comfortable and easy to be in our strength zone, and we can be heroes, which is hard to let go. This is again where being aware of when we might be overusing our strengths or overperforming can help us connect back to our intention of who we want to be in the moment.

Whether it is assuming a role, protecting our brand, or playing to our strengths, we can acknowledge that our identity is a construct of many parts. Once we understand this, then we can be more aware when there are tensions between identities that could be detracting from our overall well-being intentions. For example, one client always wanted to be seen as helpful, even if the added stress was to his own health detriment. Another client wanted to be seen as a well-thought-out expert in her craft, even if it meant spending extra hours providing backup information that may never be requested.

While these identities have likely served us well in the past, the key is to recognize the various parts of ourselves that make up our whole. This awareness allows us to make more conscious choices about which aspect of ourselves should take the lead in any given situation. Our roles and work styles are just one aspect of who we are, and we are constantly evolving. And sometimes we may need to be intentional about outgrowing our old self, taking new actions that reinforce a future-state identity.

Values: What do I care about most?

Our identities or parts are often shaped by our values. Values are core beliefs that govern our attitudes and behaviors. Sometimes values can also be in tension, and we may then feel stuck deciding the best actions to take. For example, I value my family time and I also value challenging work. I value my health, and I also value my friendships. How do we make time for all the important things? It's especially difficult when work is emailing 100 times a day with requests, and my personal health doesn't call to remind me to go to the gym. (But more on that when we get to the habits section). And it can be even more challenging when we have competing responsibilities—ask any parent or caregiver.

One tension I frequently experience is my value of being a good mom pushing up against my value of being a productive employee. Being mindful of this friction, I often notice the intersection of values and needs. Values tend to be long-term beliefs that guide our decisions. My value of being a good mom led me to make the decision to work part-time. Whereas needs are more likely to change depending on our context and life-stage. For example, recognition can be a need, and I found that sometimes in tension with my good mom values.

When my kids were young, it felt like there was a lot more recognition at work. I felt smart, helpful and rewarded for my expertise. I didn't always feel like I knew what I was doing as a parent, and let's be honest, who really does? But noticing that recognition was a need for me helped me tune into why I wasn't showing up as the mom I wanted to be. How could I make motherhood feel less thankless? By creating that awareness, I could look for new aligned ways to get my needs met. So, the next time I was stuck in a child's bedroom for hours at night, I could recast that as my child's desire to be with me because I made her feel safe and loved. Even without actual recognition, I could read into her behavior that I was living my value of being a good mom. It was important for me to reframe bedtime from a task preventing me from getting my "real" work done. I could feel appreciated for just my presence and connection, allowing me to connect to both my values and needs.

Values also influence how we approach our work, sometimes causing tension or conflict with others who hold different values. I see this a lot when I run DiSC[42] or Insights[43] work-style sessions with teams. When I ask people with different work styles to share some of their hot buttons, inefficiency comes up every time. While that is no doubt universally annoying, the "why" behind the annoyance often differs by work style. People with a strong value around action orientation and moving fast get annoyed largely because inefficiency slows things down. In comparison, people with a value around accuracy are more aggravated because inefficiency may reflect that the quality is not up to par. Understanding the value behind the trigger can help you find a way forward, whether that's reducing the annoyance or addressing the issue by making your requests known.

Closing

There's no one right answer, and tradeoffs must be made daily. However, staying attuned to emotions as signals of our needs, identity, and values can bring them into focus. Once we make them clear to ourselves, we can explore new ways to align them. This approach also helps us confront our fears, counteracting the internal judge that tries to protect us from uncertainty while keeping us stuck in old patterns.

This clarity also allows us to communicate more readily with others, enhancing trust and collaboration with our team members. It also encourages others to honor the parts of ourselves that need support, fostering a greater sense of belonging. As we saw in a previous chapter, those who feel a sense of belonging experience less burnout. By doing this internal work, you can identify more choices for yourself and gain support from others. Imagine how much more productive we could all be if every team member embraced this!

Chapter highlights:

- Start by exploring your needs. There are multiple frameworks to help you identify what your must-haves are to live a satisfactory life.
- Look at the various aspects of your identity, which may consist of your role, qualities, and/or strengths that define you.

- Values are core beliefs that govern attitudes and behaviors. Often these help you to make decisions that feel aligned with what you believe in.
- Tensions can exist within all of these, and sometimes tradeoffs need to be made. But gaining clarity on what is most important can also help you uncover new possibilities as well.

And...ACTION! Simple tools and practices to play with:

1. Capture your Big 3 Drivers at work. What needs must be met to give you work satisfaction? If they aren't currently met, think of three new ways to help you meet them, either within or outside of formal work. Example: My 3 "I's": Impact, Intellectual challenge and adult Interaction. Check out this list[44] of common needs with the Non-Violent Communication Academy if you need a place to start.

2. Practice being with two truths at once related to your needs, identity, or values. Consider what feelings and ideas emerge by exploring any tensions between them. Bonus points: What can you do differently to support holding these together versus only making tradeoffs? Some examples:
   a. I am grateful for what I have, AND I still am ambitious.
   b. I am a lawyer AND a parent.
   c. I value my health, AND I value family time.

3. Explore the various parts of your identity. Journal if helpful.

    a. What roles do you play? Which is your favorite?

    b. What do people know you for?

    c. What do you keep to yourself that others may not know about you?

    d. How much time a day do you spend in each role?

    e. Check out my more robust persona exercises on my website, www.workinghelltoworkingwell.com. Have fun with it!

4. Get clear on your strengths. What gifts or strengths can you bring to light more? You can take the CliftonStrengths[45] Assessment if you need some language or options to help. It is even better to do this with your team and reinforce the strengths you see in one another. As an alternative to the assessment, try to pause three times a day for a week or more and just notice what strengths you might be using in that moment. Remember, a strength can be knowing when to relax and regroup (for all you "More is Better" friends!).

5. When you notice there might be a tension in your values, pause and check in with your body. Where do you feel the tension? What do you make of it? Some clients have told me that they feel their throats close up when they are experiencing an integrity conflict. Others have shared they notice a heaviness to their feet as if they are being stepped on. The interpretation is up to you, but by noticing and mapping bodily sensations, you can respond more thoughtfully and quickly.

CHAPTER 5

The behaviors supporting
my ways of being

"One's character is composed of dispositions
solidified out of roles that have become habitual.
This is my *identity,* from the Latin *identidem,*
which means 'over and over.'" —David R. Loy.

Job descriptions often outline core responsibilities, yet two
people in the same role can approach their work and achieve
results in entirely different ways. And what a wondrous
discovery that is—there are so many paths to our destination!
We got to where we are for any number of reasons—our
upbringing, our first work experiences, our personal values, and
more. But what shapes our behaviors, and what keeps us stuck
in patterns we'd prefer to change?

Noticing habits

The first place we can look is our habits. What is a habit?
A habit is a routine of behavior that is repeated regularly and
tends to occur subconsciously. For example, the more hours a
day we focus on writing, the more we feel like we ARE a writer.
James Clear, in his book *Atomic Habits*[46], shares[47] "The ultimate
form of intrinsic motivation is when a habit becomes part of
your identity. It's one thing to say I'm the type of person who
wants this. It's something very different to say I'm the type of

person who is this." Sometimes, we might tell ourselves a story that gets in the way of our creating a new habit. An easy way to spot these stories is by noticing the use of the terms "I'm not" or "I'm bad at...". We are letting a current identity get in the way of creating a new identity for ourselves. Imagine what would have happened with this book if I kept telling myself, "I'm not a writer." Over time I would likely prioritize less and less time for writing, reinforcing that belief.

Now, think about the last time you successfully created a new habit. What supported you?

- Mind:
  - Observed a belief holding me back, e.g., "I'm not a morning person."
  - Used data to track progress, e.g., app, Smart Watch data, weight lifted, etc.
  - Visualized new life area upon achieving the goal
- Heart:
  - Had an accountability partner or coach cheering me on
  - Completed a new habit with a friend, e.g., running buddy
  - Enjoyed special rewards when meeting the goal and celebrated with pride, e.g., a new dress for losing weight
- Body:
  - Felt more relaxed/at ease
  - Had more energy
  - Slept better

Some habits become self-reinforcing because they make us feel noticeably better—like adopting a gluten-free diet. To maintain these habits, we might enlist additional support, such as buying a gluten-free cookbook. When deeper identity shifts are part of the change, working with a therapist or trusted friend may be necessary to sustain those habits.

At the same time, paying attention to our habits can also reveal underlying tensions. Staying curious about what's keeping our actions misaligned with our intentions is key. Creating "yes...and" statements can help us acknowledge these tensions. For example, "I love sugary treats, AND I am a healthy person who takes care of herself." This perspective allows me to enjoy indulgences, like holiday treats, without guilt while trusting I'll return to healthier choices the next day. By holding both truths together, we maintain our identity and self-compassion.

The beautiful thing about habits is that we can bundle them with other existing habits. One coaching client was working on taking time to pause and breathe to support her mindfulness. I learned that she had a consistent habit of getting herself tea between meetings. To remind her to use that time to take a breath, we experimented with putting a sticky note on her tea canister that said, "Breathe." That little visual cue was enough to help her at least breathe more life into her self-care routine. I also appreciate that bundling habits can help strengthen positive behaviors one step at a time. After adding the breath felt effortless; she could have bundled again to add a quick self-reflection check-in, such as, "How do I feel right now?" The sticky notes may run out of space eventually, but tiny changes in your day can add up.

Another client was unhappy with her habit of eating most meals at her desk while working. Through our discussions, she realized that a few underlying beliefs were influencing her behavior. She was a fabulous manager who deeply cared about her team, which translated to feeling like she had to be available to them at all hours. Wanting to balance her day with a little more self-care, we crafted a simple experiment of setting her devices to Do Not Disturb mode and giving her permission to have a 30-minute lunch break. Note the wording there. She gave herself permission. Often, we forget to give ourselves permission until we notice the identity or values manifesting as tension—I'm accessible to my team, AND I need to practice self-care. The experiment left her feeling rejuvenated for the rest of the day and more connected to her husband, who also joined her for lunch! Additionally, she set an example of healthy habits for her team, contributing to a healthier work environment for everyone.

Our habits are unique to us, but there are some commonalities in how we manage them. Gretchen Rubin, author of *The Four Tendencies*[48], describes[49] that our behavior may stem from how we respond to inner and outer expectations. "We all face two kinds of expectations—outer expectations (meet work deadlines, answer a request from a friend) and inner expectations (keep a New Year's resolution, start meditating). Your response to expectations determines your 'Tendency.'" In better understanding our tendencies, we can shine a light on what can support our habit creation or modification. For example, I tend to respond more to outer expectations than those I set for myself. So, when the pandemic hit, I became more attached to my Fitbit. While it wasn't an actual drill sergeant, it did act as an accountability partner. To get more steps, I created the habit of walking meetings with whoever would allow me to take them on the road. The beauty of that practice is that other people would sometimes take the call while walking, too. This is another example of how we can support our collective well-being by modeling positive habits.

In this section, I emphasized health examples because they're universal, easy to grasp, and often the first things we sacrifice. However, our overall well-being affects every aspect of our lives, so I encourage you to start there as a straightforward way to create more work-life harmony. Remember, good health doesn't require running a marathon—you define the habits. The key is to gain clarity on what works for you and commit to it consistently.

Expanding energy

Although building new habits won't add more hours to your day, you can experiment with managing your energy levels. By practicing mindfulness, you might find yourself feeling better about how you spend your time and doing so in a way that preserves your energy. In his book *Love + Work*[50], Marcus Buckingham's research has found that "to be fully engaged and committed to your job you don't need to love every minute of it. The magic number is 20%. If you're doing something you love at least 20% of your time, you'll like your job and want to stay in it." And hopefully you can avoid the contagious burnout that brings others down with you. Finding even a bit more meaning and satisfaction at work can create more energy for the relationships and activities we cherish most.

While there are only 24 hours in a day, there can be seemingly infinite ways to create more capacity through energy. Sleep and exercise are the common ones that most merit anyone who is struggling with burnout. The Energy Project[51] works with companies, teams, and individuals to "fuel better." Their research[52] shows that "human beings perform best and most sustainably when we move rhythmically between the expenditure of energy and the intermittent renewal of energy-physically, emotionally, mentally, and spiritually." Tuning into the energy spent or created in any time increments can be a helpful tool in creating work-life harmony.

When I look at my productive, sustainable energy at work specifically, I see that I am drawn to different energy sources, which I call the 3Cs: Creative, Connection, and Completion. An activity may generate multiple types of energy or focus on just one, but there's usually something that fuels and nourishes me when I'm in any of these energy zones at work. Each of us may experience these energies in different orders or amounts.

C1: Creative energy

This energy is admittedly a bit messy for me. It's a place where I find myself most in a flow state, and I easily lose track of time and feel bursts of creativity surge through my body. No matter what I'm doing in this zone, I tend to feel excited and energized. I can also find myself in a curiosity loop here. For instance, I might read an article that links to another, which then reminds me of a book I read last year, sparking connections between the ideas. This act of reflective sensemaking is supremely creative for me.

Now I have had the tremendous fortune to work with a lot of traditionally creative people in my life. Whether they were a toy designer, a scientist or a brilliant marketer, there was still a juicy creativity to their work. I believe that everyone has inherent creativity, and whatever that is, it must get out of us. Author and researcher Brené Brown says[53], "Unused creativity isn't benign. It lives within us until it is expressed, neglected to death, or suffocated by resentment and fear." While our unique creativity may not get airtime in a traditional work environment, I find that if we make space for this, it will fuel other parts of our lives. In their book *Your Brain on Art*[54], Ivy Ross and Susan Magsamen have shared the countless ways that the arts increase well-being, productivity, and innovation. Whether it's listening to music while you work, visiting art museums regularly, or adding a fun slide to a presentation, nurturing your creativity can be a powerful source of sustainable energy. Sharing this creativity with others can also inspire them to tap into their own, fostering deeper connections with colleagues and creating safe spaces for self-expression and idea-sharing.

CREATIVE PROCESS

1. This is awesome
2. This is tricky
3. This is shit
4. I am shit
5. This might be OK
6. This is awesome

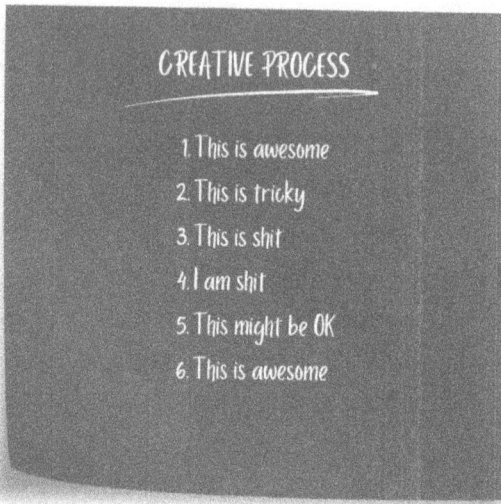

Caption: This is how I feel sometimes going through the creative process.

C2: Connection energy

I look at this kind of energy in the most expansive way possible. First, it may look like a soul connection with an old friend or a colleague who just makes us feel sane and seen. Given the loneliness epidemic, we can't lose sight of the fact that we need to be intentional about making time and space for building relationships. And based on how much time we spend there, work can be a place where we make dear and lifelong friends. I am a big believer in flexible work arrangements and know that we can still find ways to collaborate and build trust without having to be at the office five days a week. Some of my dearest friends are global colleagues who I met in person three or four times, but we intentionally created ways to connect through our love of the work we did and by sharing more of ourselves. The mythical water cooler is just one way to create a connection, but we don't need to build everything around it.

Feeling connected to the world around us can be another powerful source of energy. For example, taking walks in nature helps me feel part of a bigger picture—my body feels expanded, sometimes even tingly, and my heart fills with emotions like joy or curiosity. This sense of connection can also come from knowing I'm making an impact on the world. That might mean contributing to my organization's goals, supporting a specific population like children or people living with cancer, or creating space to give back to my community. Each of these connections fuels a deeper sense of purpose and energy.

Before you start looking at this as a to-do exercise, I want to differentiate this as intentional time focused on connecting, which is more about being than doing. For example, I do the weekly grocery shopping for my family. While I may not change the time I spend on this activity, I can certainly imbue more meaning in it. First, I can reframe the activity as my way of providing nourishment to my family, connecting to my role and a higher purpose, as opposed to just referring to it as an errand. Or I can decide to get my produce from the local farmer's market, associating it with my value of supporting the community. How can we be in a relationship with the world or people around us in a way that helps us feel connected to meaning or our purpose, big "P" or little?

C3: Completion energy

For our "check-listers," crossing something off the to-do list is amazingly satisfying. Completion, especially of challenging tasks, also ties to our feelings of self-efficacy and empowerment. I know I feel a release or quick energy rush in my body when I finish something. There even may be a feeling of contentment or pride, depending on the task. That completion energy also doesn't have to come from work alone. When people started working from home, employers would passive-aggressively joke about people doing laundry in between calls. I say amazing! Completion can be an infusion of energy! Obviously, you can't do laundry for 8 hours, but that mini break may help create space for renewal and fresh mental energy for the work at hand.

There is an intersection between completion energy and feelings of autonomy. This is why organizations that run very inefficiently can also be incredibly draining on people. It feels like you just can't get something done no matter how hard you try. Or perhaps your efforts feel so far away from the goal it's hard to see your contribution to the outcomes. For example, a friend of mine worked on a global hunger initiative. Despite the deep sense of purpose, it was challenging not to feel overwhelmed by the scale of the task and question how her individual efforts influenced such a complex system. Without regular opportunities to see even small impacts, even the most passionate individuals can begin to feel disconnected, unmotivated, or even discouraged. Breaking the work into smaller, measurable goals or redefining success through alternative metrics can help maintain focus and motivation.

Leaders and managers can play a crucial role by helping team members see their contributions, connecting the dots, and acknowledging their efforts.

Energies combined or separate:

As we're being mindful of all our patterns on this journey, it can be helpful to also notice the energy flow when the three are intermingling. What is your energy makeup for a very good day? Do you feel more courageous, even powerful? If an energy feels low, can you lean into another one? When I hit a creative block while writing this, I turned to connection or completion energy to maintain my overall momentum and stay in a productive mindset.

This is also a reminder that we don't have to navigate these moments alone—we can support one another and tap into the energy sources we need to keep going. For example, I used to run a leadership development program that had a late afternoon cohort. People often joined the virtual room feeling drained or stretched thin. Yet, in our 90 minutes together, we were usually able to transform that energy by fostering connections with one another and engaging in a shared growth experience.

Group learning environments aren't the only places where energy gets exchanged amongst participants. For example, crisis can be very appealing. All three energies are merging—likely some challenge needs creative problem solving that we can't possibly tackle alone, and it may have an urgent timeline. Adrenaline rushes may FEEL good, but as discussed earlier in the book, if we are always in that state, it can impact our health and well-being in the long term. It's essential to stay mindful of whether our energy is being used productively and sourced sustainably.

Lately, I've been paying attention to how people answer the question, "How are you?" When the response is "Busy, crazy as always," I find myself staying curious about how that makes me feel. I want to empathize and offer support, but when it's the same answer every time, I'm often at a loss for words. Sometimes, it even stirs up my own thoughts, like, "Am I busy enough? Is it okay to feel content or fully alive? Or am I not doing enough to prove my worth?" (Because more is always better, right?!) It can also be tempting to fall into a "misery loves company" dynamic, whether by bonding through shared frustrations or joining in complaints out of fear of feeling excluded. In contrast, one leader shared with me that she proactively tried to change her responses from "crazy busy" to "having fun" and noticed people responded to her positivity differently. The language we use can create a viral response in others. So, before we respond automatically to social nicety, it can be helpful to consider what energy we want to spread.

Defining boundaries

There may come a time when we need to establish boundaries around certain behaviors to safeguard our time, energy, and personal well-being. Boundaries help us teach others how to treat us by communicating what is acceptable behavior. One insight into boundaries is that they can be both rigid and flexible. For instance, I might state that I need to end a call at a specific time, but if I allow the conversation to continue, it signals that I'm more flexible and that the hard stop isn't truly firm. In this call example, I may notice the level of anxiety I feel or my need to frequently shift in my chair. These signs can clue me into how comfortable I am with the boundary being crossed. Teaching people how to be in a relationship with you starts with understanding your own boundaries.

Start by using a scale of 1-10 to assess how distressing a particular behavior is for you. Then, reflect on why it feels that way. Does it connect to one of the core fears we discussed earlier, such as people-pleasing due to fear of rejection? Or is it rooted in a values conflict? Cultural or gender-related factors might also influence these dynamics and are worth exploring with curiosity to build empathy. For example, some of my female clients have struggled with fears of being seen as "not nice" when establishing boundaries around their workload. Identifying the root cause of the stress can bring clarity. With that understanding, you can decide whether to start a collaborative conversation aimed at finding solutions that meet everyone's needs in a more balanced and productive way.

Several of my coaching clients have faced significant challenges with bosses who disrespected their boundaries. One client expressed intense anger over her manager's actions, while another responded by shrinking into submission in similar situations. This is a very real and difficult issue. Feeling unseen or unheard—especially by someone in a position of authority— can be deeply unsettling. Regardless of how we react, it often leaves us feeling uneasy or uncomfortable, prompting us to consider the best way to address the situation.

When we feel unsafe, it can be especially hard to advocate for ourselves. In today's work environment, where in-person or social interactions with our leaders may be limited, it can be especially challenging to find effective ways to collaborate with them. By becoming more aware of our boundaries and how we're affected when they're crossed, we can more clearly express our needs. Boundaries are often thought of as keeping someone out, but we can also think about them as keeping energy in. The courage to address your boundaries may need to build up over time. It may start with a statement of advocacy versus inquiry. For example:

Advocacy option: I'll be working from home Thursday due to school events. Is there anything happening on Thursday that I should be aware of or plan for?

Inquiry option: Is it alright for me to work from home on Thursday?

Note that the advocacy option is more open-ended and can invite negotiation. Whereas just simply asking permission often results in a yes or no answer.

It can also be hard to say no to people for a variety of reasons, but that is another place with lots of opportunities to practice. You can say no to the telemarketer, the sweet little Girl Scouts selling cookies, or your teen who asked for a ride somewhere 10 minutes before they needed to go. Wherever you can practice safely first, try it out and then move into more fertile ground. You can also support others who are practicing this skill too. When someone tells me no, I applaud them (really!) for being brave and taking care of themselves and their needs. This is yet another small way we can start to create a healthier collective environment for all of us.

Closing

In this chapter, we looked at the ways we operate when we are possibly on autopilot in our behaviors. Our habits, energy, and boundaries may not be very visible to us or others until we make note of them explicitly. Recognizing and articulating these patterns brings them into focus, opening the door to new possibilities through even the smallest changes and efforts. Over time, we can explore and experiment with different ways of being and navigating the world. In an upcoming chapter, we'll explore more ways to navigate the relational aspects on the path toward making your company work for you.

Chapter highlights:

- A habit is a routine of behavior that is repeated regularly and tends to occur subconsciously. Habits become intertwined with our identity. We often need to examine our beliefs and motivations to create new habits or adjust existing ones.
- While there are only 24 hours in a day, there can be seemingly infinite ways to create more capacity through energy. I categorize work-related energies into three types, which I call the 3Cs: Creative, Connection, and Completion.
- Boundaries serve to protect our time and energy, while also guiding others on how to engage with us.

And...ACTION! Simple tools and practices to play with:

1. Pick a new habit you'd like to start. Experiment with some ways that you can make the new habit feel more connected with your identity, e.g., What would a role model for well-being do? What would a successful salesperson do?

2. Combine a habit with creative energy. Some examples:

   a. If you typically take mini coffee breaks, take a scribble pad with you to draw while you wait for coffee. Extra points for sharing your drawings with others.

   b. If you make the family lunches for the day, add a special surprise like a note, sticker, or quote.

   c. Think about your typical response to the question, "How are you?" Choose a time each day to prepare your answer for when you encounter others. This allows you to stay authentic while being mindful of how your response may impact those around you.

3. Create a list of activities that help you feel connected to the bigger picture. Set aside time on your calendar each week to engage in one of those activities. Better yet, invite others to join you.

4. Explore what constitutes completion. Consider breaking down bigger projects into chunks that warrant some form of success. Then, upon completion, you can celebrate with a break, lunch with a friend, or something more tangible.

5. Reflect on your boundaries. Use a scale of 1-10 to determine what behaviors are most important to you. Journal if helpful to observe patterns.

   a. When did you experience discomfort today? To what level?

   b. Was the discomfort related to values, identity, needs, etc.? Saying no?

   c. If a certain person challenges your boundaries, what actions might you take?

CHAPTER 6

Where do I start?

"We can't solve problems by using the same kind of thinking we used when we created them."
—Albert Einstein.

Now that you've gained insight into how you operate on autopilot or within your comfort zone, it's time to explore and experiment! This chapter focuses on taking what you've learned and identifying areas where you'd like to make shifts. The goal is to create choices and put them into action, no matter how small the step. The key is to make any action feel psychologically manageable. This might involve recognizing whether it's harder for you to stop certain behaviors or start new ones. By simply reframing your intentions, you can align your actions more naturally with your purpose, whether it's a big "P" or a small one. So, how can you create a support guide for yourself on this journey? Well, it starts with the 3Ps: Planning, Pacing, and Playing.

P1: Planning

Planning is the process of turning your goals into actionable steps. For example, losing weight may be the goal, but planning to exercise, do meal prep, and more is where it really happens. Paying attention to our mind, heart, and body can help us create more realistic plans. One of my clients had amazing execution in planning for breaks. Whether it was gardening or taking a bike ride, she was ruthless with her calendar and sticking with her plan. She knew that if she took the planned breaks, as opposed to "powering through" and working, she would come back to work with more energy and greater productivity. After all, why wouldn't we plan for our well-being with the same care and responsibility as we would for any other meeting?

Not everyone can be so ruthless, but having taken the time to know some of your mind traps or habit-creation strategies can help you realistically think through your plan. For example, if my goal is to take a proper lunch break at work, I can plan for that by putting a time block on my calendar. Now, I have ignored many a personal calendar hold in my career, so this is where you may need to phone a friend. Literally. Knowing I am less likely to cancel on a friend than myself, I can plan to invite a colleague to lunch a few days each week to stay on track. The joy and connection from sharing a meal with someone can also help ease any anxiety I might feel about stepping away from work tasks for a break. And even better, that energy is bi-directional, creating greater well-being for both parties.

But sometimes, our best-laid plans may be thwarted by our fears, keeping us stuck. The fear of inadequacy may lead us to over-commit, either taking on too much or pushing ourselves to the brink to get everything done. This, in turn, can activate a fear of failure and feelings of shame if we fall short of achieving our goals. Remember, our inner judge wants to protect us and will find excuses to stop behavior change. So, we can also go into our plans with a solid Plan B, anticipating we may get sidetracked and practicing "just enough." I might not have time for the ideal lunch break I had in mind, but even a small effort can make a difference—like taking a few minutes the night before to pack a lunch or pre-ordering office food delivery. That way, I can still feel good about eating a healthy meal instead of resorting to vending machine snacks or skipping lunch altogether. Self-compassion can give us the chance to celebrate even small wins when we might have otherwise been disappointed.

Most of us have some proverbial low-hanging fruit that we can easily start with. These don't need to be the highest priorities, but they can still make a big difference in our days. For example, one of my friends bought herself a bigger water bottle. She already carried around a water bottle during her day, so it wasn't a big behavior change that required a lot of mental gymnastics or nuanced planning (other than maybe more frequent bathroom trips). Yet that small change helped her lose weight, have more energy, and feel satisfied with her efforts, yielding results. A plan doesn't need to be a multi-page spreadsheet; it can be as simple as committing to one small action every day.

P2: Pacing

Are we running a marathon or a sprint? I believe burnout is so prevalent because we treat work like a sprint, while in reality, we're in a marathon. For those unfamiliar with running, one of the key strategies for success in any race is monitoring your pace. This often involves breaking down time-to-distance ratios, like running a 15-minute mile or a 60-second 400-meter pace. Everyone has a unique capacity for different distances, but managing your pace allows you to conserve energy and plan for the long haul.

The best athletes also know that they need to plan for downtime as well. Team Sky[55] planned with military precision for downtime for its Tour de France cyclists. This included bringing their own mattresses on the road because they knew the difference sleep could make in performance. In our always-on culture, it is easy to see how if we don't monitor our energy and create space for rest, we will burn out more quickly. Stepping away to breathe, do journal reflections, or check in with our body as we stand up and stretch allows us to notice our pace and adjust accordingly. I have now started to recognize for myself the signs that I may need to adjust my pacing. My body seems fidgety, my mind races, and I feel restless. I've found that getting some fresh air on a short walk or doing a quick task for completion energy gives me a chance to settle back into a pace that feels more relaxed and purposeful.

Aside from pacing helping us to decrease the likelihood of burnout, there are work benefits as well. For example, how many times have you completed something quickly only to find out that now there's a pause in the project? I find this is commonly caused by the need to bring in other stakeholders. It can be a vicious cycle of moving so fast that we don't take time to think through our process and build check-ins with teammates. By adjusting our pace, we can allow for better planning and more focused engagement, while also helping to prevent duplicated efforts. Building a cross-functional network (like those lunch buddies) can help you quickly identify the right people to involve. This becomes even more crucial as you advance in your career, as you'll be setting the pace for a larger part of the organization.

Another place to look at pacing is with technology. Technology can certainly help us do many things faster and more efficiently. But it can also overwhelm us with information. One statistic I heard was that most of us get more information in one day than people got in a full lifetime 700 years ago! Amy Blankson, author and co-founder of the Digital Wellness Institute[56], advises[57] employers to acknowledge that screentime isn't just a personal matter. She shares that the bounty of workplace interruptions can "significantly disrupt focus and takes away from our cognitive capacities to do impactful work." To maximize your energy and contribution, there are many simple ways to manage your digital engagement. Start small by using "Do Not Disturb" features or set a timer for news and social media scrolling to help maintain your desired pace for work.

It can also get interesting when colleagues operate at a different pace than you. I remember in my first corporate job at an advertising agency, I had a manager from New York who had a super high sense of urgency. I could tell my California chill often made him anxious. One day we were packing up ads to ship to a client and had to make the FedEx deadline (if you're under 47 years old, this will not compute). I was busy packing, and my colleague kept repeating, "We are going to get this out on time, right?!" I couldn't understand why he was on repeat. I was literally getting it done before his eyes. But then it hit me: I wasn't mirroring his same urgency on the outside! So sometimes, we need to make our pace explicit to others so we can both negotiate to get our needs met.

P3: Playing

Planning small action steps and adjusting our pacing becomes easier when we introduce an element of play. I have had the good fortune of having a dad who has always embraced play. My dad is a highly accomplished physician, but I saw and benefitted from an adult who made time for play, often with me and our family. I recognize that is not the case for many people, so you may have the extra challenge of learning how to integrate play into your adult life. But play doesn't need to take time; it can be as simple as recalibrating the way you approach your work and life. Play doesn't mean neglecting our responsibilities, but rather not taking ourselves so seriously. And playfulness has numerous health benefits, including reducing stress hormones, improving lung function, and lowering the risk of heart disease, to name a few.

As you've identified areas where you'd like to build new habits or behaviors, consider starting with where you can inject some playfulness. It could be something simple, like kicking off team meetings with a quick round of Wordle or a fun icebreaker. Imagine the shift in tone that small change could bring to a meeting and the creative energy that could emerge from the shared vulnerability of having fun together. I have a playful picture for my Zoom off-camera photo, which inevitably sparks conversation and smiles. That photo even became a part of my personal brand at work and didn't seem to go out of style for more than five years! Whether done alone or with others, adding small doses of play to your day can greatly impact your well-being.

One of my favorite leaders was incredibly playful. We had a lot of team challenges and one week, there was a competition for the most steps walked. I remember him stopping by my office and basically running in place while he asked me a question. It was hard not to laugh, and I asked him to stop so I could take the conversation somewhat seriously (and not get nauseous). He also added 7 minutes of chit-chat to open every team meeting agenda so we could connect as humans and settle in. One day, he started our one-on-one meeting with his usual question, "Are you having fun?" That day, however, I broke down in tears because I was truly not enjoying my job. He then worked with me to refine my role, helping me rediscover more joy, meaning, and, of course, fun.

Learning environments are also great places to practice play. As I've created leadership programs, I always try to bring as much play as possible into the design. Doing so makes it safer to not be perfect at something new. Play serves as a great antidote for fear of failure, keeping us in a space of curiosity and exploration as opposed to performance and achievement. If we are growing and developing in our career, most of us will be in a learning mode at least some of that time. While it may be uncomfortable not to know something, play can create a counterbalance and return our nervous system to a homeostasis level.

Another place to explore play is an area where you might start a sentence with, "I'm not good at...." There may be a self-limiting belief to investigate there. For example, one of the requirements of my coaching certification program was having a meditation practice. Now, I am the person sitting next to you at the movies, fidgeting the whole time, so sitting still for any number of minutes was very daunting to me at the outset. I kept trying, getting frustrated and then down on myself in a constant loop. But then it hit me! I was trying to PERFORM meditation. Once I realized that, I shifted to a place of experimentation and playfulness that allowed me to truly have meditation practice. I am no Dalai Lama, but I have found tremendous benefits from even just enough meditation and not looking at it as something to be achieved.

Play is also an opportunity to practice a growth mindset, a term coined by Dr. Carol Dweck, professor and author. She says[58], "The growth mindset is based on the belief that your basic qualities are things you can cultivate through your efforts. Although people may differ in every which way in their initial talents and aptitudes, interests, or temperaments, everyone can change and grow through application and experience." A growth mindset keeps learning at the center, and challenges are just a way to keep growing. The simplest way to practice a growth mindset is to notice the inner judge, or outer voice for that matter, saying, "I don't know how to..." or "I'm not good at...." Then you end that sentence with a "yet." It's an incredibly powerful reminder of our ability to develop and evolve as people. Once your team knows to add this word, it is also a powerful way to support others in their growth too. When I am feeling unsure of my ability to do something, it always brings a smile to my face when a friend uses that not-so-secret code to remind me that I just don't know how to do it "yet."

Closing

Again, the spirit of this book is to support you in creating action to live your best and most sustainable life (or at least get an hour in your week back for some joy!). The 3 Ps give you just a few places to consider where to get started on your journey. When we create more choices for ourselves, we are better able to align our attention with our intentions. Thoughts do have the power to shape our experiences. And research[59] has shown that if we feel like we are in control of how we perceive stress, our bodies are less likely to see it as harmful and burnout. No matter where you choose to begin, I'm confident you'll find a small step to take and continue building over time as you wish.

Chapter highlights:

- This chapter is a support guide to getting you started on your well-being journey by using the 3Ps: Planning, Pacing, and Playing.
- Planning is actioning your goals, e.g., losing weight is the priority, but planning to exercise, meal prep, and more is where it really happens. In a way, starting with the actions we are willing to take helps us reverse engineer our priorities.
- Are we running a marathon or a sprint? Without considering our pacing, we may be ripe for burnout. Noticing our physiological needs, staying connected cross-functionally, and monitoring our digital wellness are all ways to pace ourselves appropriately.

- Play serves as a great antidote for a fear of failure, keeping us in a space of curiosity and exploration as opposed to performance and achievement.

And...ACTION! Simple tools and practices to play with:

1. Start by setting aside 5 minutes a day for well-being planning. This is far less than the time you would set aside for a meeting. It could be for anything. Some ideas:
    a. Quick journal entry on gratitude and hopes for the day
    b. Rescheduling a meeting to meet co-workers for lunch
    c. Deciding on the home yoga video to try the next day
2. Celebrate clarity and growth. One client started making an "Aligned Actions to my Intentions" list at the end of the day to recognize herself for living according to her own values and vision. Acknowledging what you have done creates more self-compassion for not "doing" everything and getting stuck in the "shoulds."
3. Start recognizing your pacing preferences and needs. What is your magic formula for maintaining your marathon energy?
4. Analyze your stakeholder network. What groups or teams touch your work? Do you know what their priorities and obstacles are? Once you've done the analysis, consider ways to build out your network further with check-ins. For a stakeholder analysis template, go to www.workinghelltoworkingwell.com.

5. Pick a new activity to practice play and practice a beginner's mindset[60]. Learn how to play mahjong. Pick up a ukulele. Find a pickleball game. Or dust off the bike and put air in the tires. Then, find a new trail to explore. The cadence is up to you but try for at least weekly. Think of it as practicing for retirement.

6. Create a quarterly team challenge around well-being. Some ideas:

   a. Steps challenge

   b. Lunchtime Uno tournament

   c. Loudest Leaver award—best dramatic exits!

CHAPTER 7

Bringing others with you on the journey

"A rising tide lifts all the boats."
—John F Kennedy.

Changing mindsets and behaviors is hard. We really need the support of others in some shape or form to be able to practice the elegant dance of work-life harmony. Your needs will be unique to you, but simply recognizing the interconnected web we all live and work within can be valuable.

Building a supportive core

First, it is helpful to think through who is in your support network. They may sit both in and outside of work. And they may not always be telling you what you want to hear. It's important to recognize that a support network isn't always made up of cheerleaders; it can include truth-tellers as well—and sometimes the truth can sting. When my 12-year-old told me that I was on autopilot and addicted to my phone and never really listened to her...ouch, that hurt a lot. But it was a wake-up call that one of the most important people in my life was experiencing me that way. Of course, I had a choice to take that as an opportunity for reflection and action or just ignore it. Telling the truth, especially when it's difficult, is an act of care. It can be helpful to remember this, even when our heart hurts.

In the same spirit of care, I have greatly benefitted from working both with managers and team members who approach work differently than I do. Often, I tend to get excited about a lot of things, and for better or worse, I can be a bit of a time optimist. So, having a leader or team member to run an idea by has often protected me from myself. There is such a gift in genuinely asking, "Is this really worth your time?" or "Do you think people really have the capacity for that now?" Having people who can say no with care not only challenges us to think more intentionally but also reminds us of the importance of leaning on others for support.

After all, achieving work-life harmony becomes even harder when we struggle to ask for or accept help. With many of my clients, I have observed their feeling that they are all alone in their hero's journey. Whether that looks like delegating work or using someone else's project plan as a foundation for your own--you may need to lean on others more than you have in the past. It might not be comfortable to ask for support, but it may be the only way to get your needs met. And it's also useful to be mindful of how you receive help. Imagine if my husband washed all the dishes after a dinner party, and then I promptly removed them to wash them again. How likely would he be to help next time?

Sometimes, we tell ourselves stories about what will happen if we ask people for support. A team I was coaching had a hard time holding each other accountable because they felt bad asking for deliverables on the agreed-upon deadline, not wanting to stress their busy peers further. In another instance, one of my coaching clients had anxiety about letting people down. When she was offered an opportunity on a new project she was genuinely excited about, she felt guilty leaving her current manager with the existing work, so she didn't end up taking it. Empathy for others is important, but I've learned that many people are eager to lend a hand and are willing to help, even when their own schedules are full. If you've created a safe space for people to say no or negotiate, then it makes it easier to ask because you know they will be honest about their bandwidth.

Taking time to have discussions with managers, team members, and partners in advance can feel awkward but it helps when the sticky situations come around. If you are planning to shift how you're working now, you may need to set expectations accordingly with people who rely on you for support. Conversely, you can also set the stage for greater comfort in future conversations. I know some of my team members would squirm at first when I would proactively say to them, "I know I won't get to keep you on my team forever, so what can I do to support your growth now? What roles will you be looking for in the future? I am here to support you as a person, not just when you are on my team." Conversations like this open the door to transparency and real communication about ways we can support one another, whether it is professionally or personally. Any one of us can start these kinds of conversations, and it may take courage. But you may be pleasantly surprised by what comes back.

Expanding networking

Let's just start with the potential resistance here. Networking feels icky to some people. I get it. The ick often comes from the narrative that you are shamelessly self-promoting or kissing up to superiors in the hopes of getting special treatment. Some people don't like networking because the power differential feels uncomfortable as if they have nothing to offer a more established or senior person. And others don't want to network until they have their story and everything else figured out first. That's a lot of energy spent fighting something with a rather innocuous definition. Networking can be defined as "a supportive system of sharing information and services among individuals and groups having a common interest." If you are one of the people who resist networking, how could this neutral definition support how you might find a new mindset with some comfortable actions to take?

There can be so many beautiful connections to be built and shared. I like taking an expanded view of networking as well. Networking can truly be done with anyone—up, down, across, inside, or outside. You can go deeper with some people, or you can operate in the spirit of five-minute favors[61] (the basis for Reid Hoffman's founding LinkedIn). What I love about five-minute favors is that they are not only easy to find the time for but also feel good. For those who are more service-oriented, it can be helpful to view networking as not only benefiting yourself but also enhancing your ability to assist and support others. You can also start small. If you have ten strong connections and each one of them has ten strong connections, you can easily access 100 people without too much stress.

However you decide to build your network, it is a worthwhile investment. We all have something to give, and there will always be a flow between giving and receiving support from your network over the long term.

Within organizations, networking also allows you to create a more complete picture of the bigger priorities around you. As I shifted to part-time hours, I felt incredibly grateful for the relationships I had built in the past few years, as they enabled me to "phone a friend" to better understand what was happening elsewhere in the company. Through even short conversations, I could build more empathy for other people's drivers, needs, and challenges. And then, I could prioritize my work and projects to better align across the organization not to be either isolated or disconnected.

Staying in the loop can also present opportunities for looking at your workload differently. For example, it can present a chance for co-creation where you might be able to partner with someone working on something similar. It can also catch possible duplication of effort, especially in larger organizations where communication channels may run less efficiently. Or it can help you find time-saving work that already exists, possibly modifying your own deliverables. Lastly, you can identify stakeholders or allies that can help with any change management needed, hopefully protecting you from re-work. Like everything else, your network only works if you work it. Even my most time-starved clients were able to find 30 minutes a month to focus on networking and some even more. There is nothing to lose by asking, and people might pleasantly surprise you with their response!

Courageous negotiating

I've seen the pain and burden of just continuously adding on to people's plates. "We must do more with less!" is too often the rallying cry. Then, when fears or work addiction go unchecked, we still kill ourselves to get it all done, which then just serves to reinforce the overloading behavior. While I do believe it is the organization's responsibility to plan for demands and resources, some of us are in organizations that don't do that effectively yet. So, you may need to be the brave trailblazer to encourage that kind of negotiating in your organization.

As you begin changing the way you work, be mindful of how it might affect those around you. More work could be shifted to others, and they may not be thrilled about it. To avoid resentment, negotiate upfront and involve them in finding a win-win solution that benefits everyone's well-being. This approach can position you as a role model, but it might also lead to unforeseen challenges if you don't clarify your intentions. While you can't control how your manager or colleagues will respond, knowing their needs and aspirations (thanks to your networking) can help. Start by viewing your workload through a developmental lens—are there tasks that could offer growth opportunities for others? If so, consider how to delegate them, positioning yourself as a coach or mentor rather than just an executor.

Another avenue to prepare for a bargaining discussion is by taking a project management approach. If your workload increases or needs to be scaled back, one way to negotiate a more manageable balance is by evaluating the impact on time, quality, or cost of other, potentially higher-priority tasks. Here's how you could approach the conversation with your manager from an advocacy perspective:

> *You:* I'm really excited about this new report and think the data shared can really impact our business. To give me more time to focus on the new report, I'd like to produce my other customer report quarterly instead of monthly.

> *Manager:* But people expect that report monthly, so I don't think that will work.

> *You:* I think if I can reduce the time on the current report, I will have more time to make the new report better quality and possibly reduce the need for the old report.

> *Manager:* Of course, I want the new report to be great. I just think you can manage both, given your skills.

> *You:* I hear your discomfort with letting the old report go. I'd suggest that we maybe skip one month to give me time to focus on the new report and then we can revisit to see if there was a lot of noise around the missed report. If that doesn't feel comfortable, maybe we can look at other projects that could be delegated or delayed. I want to keep doing great work on this team.

End scene.

Of course, this conversation could go back and forth like a tennis match for much longer. By advocating for some possible solutions, reflective of time and then quality here, you can get out of the yes/no binary situation that sometimes permission asking creates. This sets you up not just for new possibilities but also to hear more about a decision-maker's priorities, preferences, and flexibility.

It does take courage to advocate for your needs and wants. But you may also need to take stock of your boundaries. As the saying goes, "If you want something done, give it to the busiest person." But that busy person may really want to say no, and you may BE that busy person. So, getting clear on your boundaries can also help you get more comfortable with saying no or negotiating. One place to start is reflecting on times when you do let your boundaries get crossed.

- Is it a who, e.g., a senior-level person or your work bestie?
- Is it a when question, e.g., morning requests are harder to say no to than early evening ones?
- Is it a what question, e.g., a highly visible project with important stakeholders?

Whatever your reason for letting your boundaries relax, sometimes acknowledging the tradeoffs or costs to your well-being can spark more courage. Or practice a powerful body shape and let your body support you!

Another way to look at negotiating is that it is just communicating to gain greater clarity. There doesn't need to be a win-lose or yes/no situation. One way to do that is to ask more questions and even request more time before agreeing to the request. Using my family airport departure example from a previous chapter, that might start with some basics like:

1. What actions should be taken? E.g., We need to pack, lock up the house, take out garbage, etc.
2. Who will do what? E.g., I will pack the bags if you feed the kids.
3. What is the expected timing? E.g., Some actions will be taken a couple of days prior and some the day of departure.
4. What are the conditions of fulfillment (directional or complete)? E.g., We will be all ready to walk out the door at 7:45 am or at least call a ride share by that time.
5. Is there a network of support or stakeholders to engage? E.g., Nana can pick us up.

Then, you might ask if you can get back to the person with additional thoughts. Of course, you will need to follow up. And when you do, you can follow a similar project management approach as above by sharing what will shift to time, cost or quality for you to take on the work. (E.g., If we buy breakfast at the airport, it may cost more, but there will be less stress that morning.) This closes the circle of communication to gain greater clarity for all parties and further sustain a strong relationship.

Closing

This chapter has been about ways to bring others on your journey to greater well-being. As the world gets increasingly complex, I believe that we can't do everything ourselves. There is too much information, too much distraction, and too much work needed for any one of us to go it alone. By integrating a supportive core, we have more hands to hold it all. As we build out our network, we can find new avenues for getting work done and focus on what is most important. Then, by honing our negotiating skills, we can advocate for the options that are most purposeful for us while staying true to our needs and boundaries. It won't happen overnight, but allowing ourselves to build a human web around our work can create a cushion within the complexity.

Chapter highlights:

- Consider who is in your support network. They may sit both in and outside of work. And they may not always be telling you what you want to hear.

- Networking is "a supportive system of sharing information and services among individuals and groups having a common interest." If you are one of the people who resist networking, how could this neutral definition support how you might find a new mindset with some comfortable actions to take?

- Within organizations, networking also allows you to create a more complete picture of the bigger priorities around you. Staying in the loop can also present opportunities for looking at your workload differently, with the potential for co-creation or minimizing duplicative effort.

- I've seen the pain and burden of just continuously adding on to people's plates. "We must do more with less!" is too often the rallying cry. Finding the courage to negotiate may take time but there are multiple avenues to explore. Focusing on development needs, using a project management approach, and being mindful of your boundaries can all bring greater clarity, leading to more effective outcomes.

And...ACTION! Simple tools and practices to play with:

1. Make a list of colleagues and friends who tell you "No." Seek them out more frequently to support your work-life harmony goals. Just by helping you refine even one thing, they may save you much time or energy.

2. Practice five-minute favors. One of the easiest ones is introducing people to other people. Sharing a relevant article or sample piece of work are two other easy ones. Once you start doing it more, you'll find more opportunities to do it as it gets easier and more rewarding.

3. Block 30 minutes a month on your calendar for networking calls or coffee. It can be within your organization or outside. If you're struggling with motivating yourself to network, check out my "4 Networking Beliefs to Get You Unstuck Guide" on www.workinghelltoworkingwell.com.

4. Look at your current workload with a developmental lens. Is there someone else who would be able to learn and grow from delegating some work to them?

5. Play with your body shapes. What gives you courage and helps you feel strong and centered? For fun, check out the Ted Lasso episode[62] where Rebecca "makes herself big."

6. When negotiating around a new project or work being added to your plate, consider the triple constraints of project management to create greater clarity as to how to appropriately shuffle the work.

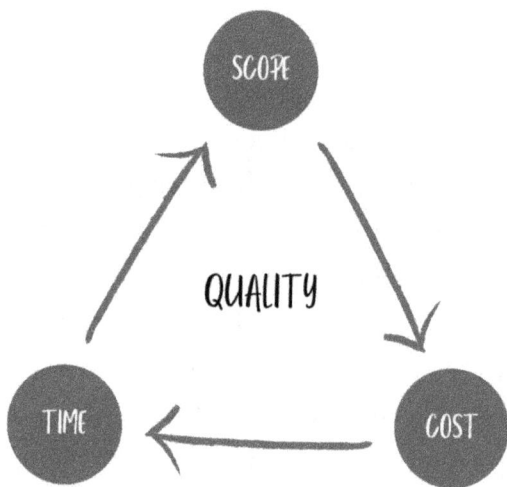

CHAPTER 8

Skills for people leaders

"The true price of leadership is the willingness
to place the needs of others above your own.
Great leaders truly care about those they are
privileged to lead and understand that the true
cost of the leadership privilege comes at the
expense of self-interest."
—Simon Sinek.

Some of you reading this book may have an additional role that you play as a leader of people. As such, you may be processing how you both apply these principles for yourself and as a leader supporting your team members. The responsibilities of people leaders will undoubtedly differ based on the scope and nature of your role, the size of your team—whether you lead them directly or indirectly—and the broader organizational expectations placed upon you. Many of you may find yourselves in player-coach roles, where you manage a smaller team while also maintaining your own deliverables and productivity targets. And this is tough. A recent Harvard Business Review article[63] noted, "more than half of managers (53%) report feeling burned out at work." Balancing the various accountabilities of a people leader presents its own challenges to mastering work-life harmony.

This chapter builds on the assumption that you've been reflecting on the earlier chapters and are motivated to amplify your leadership to promote greater well-being within your team. First, you need to make sure you are managing your own well-being. If you're stressed and exhausted, you won't have the capacity to think creatively about the work. Even with your best intentions, you may need to just focus on yourself for a while, and that is more than okay; you are still likely to have an impact on your team. Other than the obvious action of role modeling well-being practices, there are some skills you can hone when working with others.

These are generally basic management skills, but when you layer in the intention of making people's lives more harmonious with work, they take on new life. Further, the research[64] shows that a good relationship with management supports employee satisfaction and engagement, ultimately driving better business results. Below, I've tried to identify the most impactful skills that benefit from simple practice or ritual and don't need to take a lot of time. I know people leaders are often the most time-starved! As John Maxwell shared in his book, *The 21 Laws of Leadership*[65], "Leadership develops daily, not in a day."

If you're overwhelmed already, just skip to the tools and practices at the end of the chapter.

Developing talent

This is one of the most important skills in business, especially in a complex, changing environment. The beautiful thing about development is that it can get a big boost from intention and doesn't have to take a lot of leadership time. Initiating a conversation to learn about a team member's skills, motivations, passions, and desired future roles can provide valuable insight into how you can support their growth. If trust and a strong relationship are established, gaining a better understanding of their life outside of work can also be beneficial. And that can happen over time and multiple interactions. Integrating development into work expectations is likely to cultivate a greater sense of purpose and engagement among your team members, which can also lead to improved outcomes.

Becoming known as a great team leader who develops people increases the likelihood of attracting new team members both internally and externally. One way to do that is by fostering connections across the organization. It enhances your leadership impact and is a powerful way to support both individual and team development. You can negotiate for mentorship or make suggestions for networking and relationship-building. Some of my coaching clients didn't do much internal networking for fear that their manager would think they were looking for other jobs and possibly retaliate. While that may be a story that they were telling themselves, there is no benefit in team members not expanding their network. Organizations are always evolving and potentially reorganizing, so a fully connected team is likely to be more productive and resilient as team size and composition change.

Another way to plan for development is to secure some margins in the work. I know it's easier said than done, but even mentally adding a 20% buffer to your time or resources can help you plan not just for the unexpected but also to seize new opportunities. This margin allows room for skill development, collaboration on potential projects, or handling urgent requests from executives. I've seen many leaders consistently give high-visibility tasks to the same person because others aren't as skilled yet, but this can lead to burnout for top performers. Additionally, it can trigger feelings of unfairness among other team members who may feel their development is being overlooked while a favored colleague receives the best or most prestigious work. The extra buffer allows time and space for learning and coaching so special projects don't always have to go to the employee who already knows how to do it. Spreading development love around the team makes them more apt to help each other, too, resulting in greater team well-being overall.

If you need some added incentive, being a great people developer means you are more likely to have a stress-free vacation! One of my favorite "out of office" messages came from a wonderful people leader. It said, "I'll be out of the office this week. For emergencies, I can be reached by cell phone. Otherwise, I promise my team can handle it. They are pretty amazing." It's such a great way to set a tone of empowerment while also creating boundaries that open doors for others to grow. If you've fostered a team that relies on one another and is not just centered on your direction, they will also see that vacation can be an opportunity for exposure or development. This can help reduce stress on the team when anyone is on vacation, and people need to step in. By setting the tone that vacations are covered, everyone can take the time they need to recharge while others see an opportunity for growth.

As you get to know your individual team members better, you'll likely gain a clearer understanding of how to harness the strengths and address the development areas of the entire team. Many people leaders feel they must be the sole driver of development within the team. While this is an important aspect of your role, you can also operate more like a "producer"— coordinating, delegating, and planning the work—without needing to be involved in every detail. You can set the tone by encouraging team members to recognize and utilize each other's strengths and giving shout-outs to those who have contributed to their development. And you can create connections for skill-building and resilience. With this approach, you empower your team to take ownership of their growth while you guide them toward collective success.

Creating clarity

Recognizing people's growth and development is a great way to create clarity as to what good looks like. And sometimes, the clarity needed is around the best way to work with you. In the previous chapters you might have noted your values, your needs, or your identity. Sharing your preferences and leadership principles with your team members can alleviate some of their stress around making you happy or satisfied.

One way to do this for new leaders is a process called a new leader assimilation. I recall guiding a team through the process at one point. A former peer had returned to lead the team. In the discussion, the leader shared that she was trying to be respectful of how the team was working and didn't want to be the proverbial new sheriff in town. The team appreciated that she was being respectful, but they felt her hesitation and wanted more vision and direction. The leader shared with me afterward that if we had not created this space for discussion, she likely would have kept tiptoeing around the team longer, furthering their frustration around the lack of clarity. In addition to facilitating communication about how the first 60 or 90 days are progressing, new leader assimilations also provide an opportunity for constructive two-way communication. This fosters an environment where team members can assess a leader's receptivity to upward feedback, making it easier and safer for them to provide it in the future, keeping leaders better informed.

A leader in the know is better equipped to gain clarity on challenges, recognizing that issues often stem from multiple factors rather than being solely one person's fault. As the saying goes, "If you're not part of the solution, you're part of the problem." After leading a workshop on giving and receiving feedback, one participant came up to me for advice. She felt trapped in a merry-go-round conversation with her manager, who repeatedly gave feedback that she needed to check her work more. In turn, she would then convey to her manager that the timelines were too short to have time to check adequately. The employee was growing increasingly frustrated with an expectation she wasn't sure she could meet. While you can be clear in your expectations, it is important to also listen for and understand constraints for your own clarity. This opens up a richer dialogue, with less frustration for both parties, on the conditions of success and how they may be created or tempered.

While it can seem like a time-consuming task, making the time for clarity is ultimately a kind and beneficial approach for everyone involved. Clear communication helps to prevent misunderstandings and sets expectations, which in turn saves time and energy in the long run. Clarity is most effective when it's a bi-directional exchange, allowing both parties to share and understand each other's perspectives. This open flow of communication fosters better collaboration and trust. Additionally, incorporating regular mindfulness practices can enhance your ability to stay focused, calm, and regulated even in emotionally charged conversations. As a team leader, these practices can have a multiplier effect, improving both your leadership effectiveness and the overall well-being and productivity of your team.

Empathetic negotiating

Now, you have shown your team members that you care about their development. And you're trying to be as clear as possible on the work at hand and the conditions of success. So, your employees will go do what must be done perfectly, right? It can be easy to forget sometimes that your employees aren't actually corporate robots but rather human beings with free will. There will always be an element of choice and negotiation present in any interaction between two people. In addition to the skills above, being an empathetic negotiator will help you support team members in having greater work-life harmony.

At times, our own stress can distract us from maintaining the proper focus on the relationship. After another recent workshop, a participant approached me asking for insights into an interaction with his manager. He had worked a 12-hour day and didn't have time to complete a report. His manager, without acknowledging the exhausted employee in front of him, shared that he was upset the employee didn't complete the assignment he asked for. It sounded like the conversation had a lot of back and forth about the "what," but the employee was frustrated the "who" was not seen or heard. By just focusing on tasks alone, we miss an opportunity to understand the person and their values, identity, and purpose, which can ultimately support better work together. A people leader can, of course, still share their disappointment and try to figure out how to get the necessary work done. But by taking one minute to first honor and empathize with the human in front of you, you're more likely to balance the tasks with the relationship.

Another way to create empathy is by practicing full-body listening through taking in body language, emotions, as well as words. In particular, listen for needs and respect any boundaries a team member is brave enough to bring up. One of my coaching clients had a boss who never respected her clearly stated boundaries around time. Every one-on-one call ran late, despite her frequent noting that she needed to get to another obligation. One unfortunate day, my client had to make up an extreme excuse to get off the call and still unheard, literally had to hang up on her boss. There is really nothing more stressful than a boss who won't honor boundaries. When this happens, it often leads to a mindset where negotiation feels like a win-lose situation rather than an opportunity for mutual understanding and compromise.

This mindset of win-lose negotiation can be reinforced by past experiences where boundaries were not respected, shaping how we approach conflicts today. Many of us may have grown up in environments where healthy relationship negotiations weren't modeled, and we bring that baggage to work. I view negotiating as distinct from compromise, deciding what's right or wrong, or simply giving in. This starts with finding common ground, identifying gaps, and then moving away from black-and-white thinking to create solutions around those gaps.

In an effort to be solutions-oriented, one of my coaching clients proactively came up with a plan to work differently so she wouldn't be at risk of burnout. When she shared her plan with her manager, he heard her out but then wouldn't flex at all on her needs. I'd imagine he was under great unmanaged stress himself if he was unable to meet her creative solutions with an open mind. I've encountered many leaders who are empathetic to the challenges people are facing, but the key difference is in staying open to negotiation. In any relationship, being able to negotiate well is critical to the relationship's success.

A simple approach to responding to a negotiation is actually running an experiment. In the case of my client navigating burnout, her manager could have given her plan a try for two weeks with a few points of agreed-upon criteria to check back in on. Then, they could negotiate again on possible pivots. This approach would create more autonomy to be felt and actual avoidance of burnout, the original problem that got lost in discussion. If someone is brave enough to tell you they are worried about burnout, you have a narrow window to partner with them to course correct before you have an unintended opening.

Another reframe for negotiating is looking at it as thought-partnering. Let your employees think out loud with you, sharing their needs and obstacles. We all love giving advice and telling someone what to do can be "faster" than listening. Instead, how can you stay open and curious long enough to get all the information needed? You may need to notice your own assumptions and stay aware of your judgments. Share the stories rolling around in your head to clarify the odds of them coming to fruition. For example, are you coming from a place of being overprotective? Your past pain may not be theirs, and protecting them from challenge, failure, and discomfort can impede their growth. Consider how you can walk beside them in navigating their well-being needs along with the needs of the business.

Closing

If you want to play a supportive role in your team members' well-being, you will need to know the human in front of you on some level. That includes the human in the mirror. Use the 3Ps, planning, pacing, and playing, to support you in taking action. Planning could be putting 30 minutes on Friday at 2 pm for recognition emails. Pacing could be just focusing on one of the tools or suggestions and not moving to the next until the first feels integrated and automatic. Playing can look like making negotiating less scary, for example, using lighter language like gameshow analogies or sports scoring throughout a discussion.

Now, some of you may be thinking to yourself, I'm the boss, and they should do what I say. You may have the last word in this conversation, but you are setting up a power dynamic by which they may have the last word when they quit. Or worse, they have stayed and are filling valuable talent real estate but not contributing at their full potential. It's always your choice, but worth trying on a different boss style and seeing what happens.

Let's pull this through a specific example in action. You've invited an employee to fill in for you at an important meeting. You know they are trying to be mindful of self-care, and the meeting conflicts with their weekly pilates session, so they will likely say no. Before you roll your eyes and get all bossypants, let's play this out. You can start the conversation by sharing that an opportunity has come up that you think would be good for their development (check). You know that it conflicts with their usual self-care routine, but if they can be flexible, you think it will be a good use of their time for a variety of reasons (Clarity). Since they would miss their normal class, let's look at ways we can move things in their schedule to attend at another time. (Negotiating). That wasn't so bad, right? They may still say no, and then you can make some other choices in your behavior, but this can give you a place to start.

I've shared lots of ideas here, and you may be feeling overwhelmed. Pick one tool or practice from below to play and experiment with. You can pick based on feedback or just where you'd notice a meaningful change in your ability to work with a growth mindset. Where is the small tweak? Where can you acknowledge you're not skilled yet? Ultimately, we're looking to shift from a common manager identity of judge to that of gardener or conductor. You have an opportunity to bring the best out in people and, most importantly, yourself.

Chapter highlights:

- First, you need to make sure you are managing your own well-being. If you're stressed and exhausted, you won't have the capacity to think creatively about the work with your team.

- Other than the obvious action of role modeling well-being practices, there are some skills you can hone to support your team: Developing Talent, Creating Clarity, and Empathetic Negotiating.

- Initiating a conversation to learn about a team member's skills, motivations, passions, and desired future roles can provide valuable insight into how you can support their growth. As you get to know your individual team members better, you will also likely see a fuller picture of how you can leverage the whole team, supporting both strengths and development areas.

- Fostering connections inside and out of your company can also support employee growth. Organizations are constantly evolving and potentially reorganizing, so a fully networked team can be more productive and resilient as team size and composition change.

- Being clear on conditions for success allows people to rise to the occasion. Clarity is best as a bi-directional conversation, recognizing different needs and obstacles. Clear communication helps to prevent misunderstandings and sets expectations, which in turn saves time and energy in the long run.
- There will always be an element of choice and negotiation present in any interaction between two people. Being an empathetic negotiator will help you support team members in having greater work-life harmony while still achieving desired business results.

And...ACTION! Simple tools and practices to play with:

1. Check out www.workinghelltoworkingwell.com for a free guide to development conversations. Use the guide to plan for a targeted meeting or to pepper into your regular one-to-one meetings. When assigning new work, tie back to development goals and skills to be gained. Brainstorm with your team members a list of people they should network with.

2. Create a two-by-two priority matrix with your team to capture all the key work and projects for the year. Once you have this list of tasks or deliverables, you then start prioritizing them based on the impact and ease of implementation axes (see visual below). This gives the team clarity as to the total work happening within the group. Then, you can discuss potential partnerships or

mentoring within the team to create more development opportunities for all.

Think of a project that you'd like to make easier or more impactful

BUSINESS IMPACT

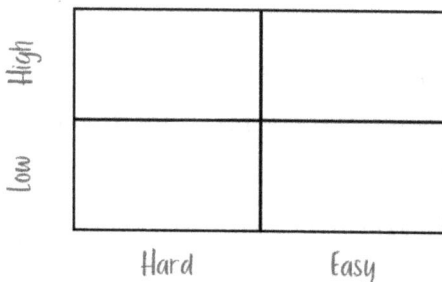

High

Low

Hard   Easy

EASE OF IMPLEMENTATION

3. Reflect on your comfort with delegating and/or asking for help. Journal if helpful to observe patterns.
   a. When did you delegate or ask for help today?
   b. Do you notice any beliefs you may have related to this? For example, "It's easier just to do it myself" or "It's ultimately my responsibility." Or "They are so busy already..."
   c. Do you notice any discomfort related to fears, values, identity, needs, or more?
4. Experiment with some listening practices for at least a week. Reflect on any changes or ask for feedback. Build

your own listening practice or borrow one of the ones below:

a. In my next 1:1 with my team members, I will paraphrase what needs, constraints, or requests I heard to confirm my understanding.

b. When asking an open-ended question, I will count to seven before responding and jumping in with the solution.

c. Practice WAIT (Why Am I Talking?) in meetings and track how many times I catch myself talking when I should be listening.

5. Allow team members to thought partner with you and run experiments around how their work gets done. It might start with finding common ground and then moving to identify the gaps. Then, shifting from black-and-white thinking to create plans around those gaps. You can invite your employees into further negotiation on the criteria to evaluate the potential pivot points.

6. Create your own recognition practice. Calendar time each week or month to recognize team members. Or practice "Thank you for...." Instead of just saying thank you, say thank you for a skill or behavior you want to reinforce. "Thank you for your patience." "Thank you for your insightful questions." "Thank you for the feedback."

CHAPTER 9

Organizational considerations

"Rather than striving to make humans better at work, organizations can make work better for humans." —Jen Fisher.

Some of you reading this book may play a role in or want to influence how well-being is addressed at an organizational level. Employee activism is on the rise, and well-being is no longer a nice-to-have. Companies that realize this sooner will have a competitive advantage and deliver more value to their stakeholders. Leadership obviously casts a big shadow on the collective well-being of an organization, but a single leader can't carry the bag alone. For this chapter, I'm going to level up work-life harmony (more individually modeled) to that of collective well-being and sustainable performance.

To achieve this, it's essential to align strategy, culture, and programs. At its core, strategy is simply a framework for making tradeoff decisions about how to compete. As AI reaches its full potential, talent will undoubtedly play an even greater role in a company's competitive edge. Therefore, ensuring employees are healthy and productive will be vital to successfully executing the company's strategy.

Culture is where strategy comes to life through execution. At its core, culture is simply how things get done—especially when no one is watching. For instance, in companies with a first-to-market strategy, you often find a "hustle" culture where deadlines, product launches, and approvals dominate. However, if demands and resources aren't balanced effectively, this can foster a culture prone to burnout, undermining sustainable performance in the long-term race for innovation. I once spoke to an employee during an exit interview who shared that she had accomplished more in two years at the company than in five years at her previous job. While this reflects incredible growth from a development standpoint, it's not ideal for the company to invest in developing talent only to lose them because they couldn't see a way to slow down to a more sustainable pace.

Lastly, programs provide a structural means to support both strategy and an aligned culture. Many organizations start here because programs often represent low-hanging fruit and are easier to implement. While it's ideal to begin with strategy, it's not necessary to abandon existing efforts entirely. The key is to evaluate how these programs align with the overall strategy and culture and ensure they are the right ones to have in place. The plans you implement will be tailored to your organization, but the World Wellbeing Movement provides a playbook with many research-backed[66] ones to help you get started.

Aligning strategy

Organizations may choose to develop a well-being strategy, which often becomes part of HR's goals. However, without proper integration and support across the organization, this can sometimes result in a narrow focus on mental health and exercise programs. While such programs have their benefits, as the earlier research[67] indicated, they are not sufficient on their own to significantly enhance employee well-being or achieve the associated business outcomes. HR can play a vital role as stewards of these efforts, but true success requires a shared sense of ownership throughout the organization.

One approach is to integrate well-being into your existing strategy. Take Airbnb, for example. In their communicated roadmap to bring magical travel to everyone[68], they outlined four strategic pillars, one of which focused on recognition and investing in the Airbnb community. Extending that concept to employees as part of the Airbnb community creates a natural synergy with a broader well-being strategy. Judging by their cultural values and high ranking on Indeed's Work Wellbeing Index[69], Airbnb seems to have successfully woven various well-being components into their strategy. This serves as a great example of how you can connect the dots at an organizational, group, or even team level.

Organizational decision-makers may need to review data from various research entities to fully understand the impact of well-being on the bottom line before committing more time and resources to an embedded strategy. While external data from organizations like the World Wellbeing Movement[70], 4 Day Week Global[71], and others can be valuable, some leaders may find internal data more compelling. Engagement surveys can be a valuable source of insights, and frameworks from organizations like Healthy Place to Work[72] highlight key levers for integrating well-being into your strategy for sustainable performance. Additionally, platforms like Indeed's Work Wellbeing Index[73] offer data tailored to your organization. Whether you're in a decision-making role or looking to influence those who are, leveraging these data sources—along with resources from the notes or the organizations mentioned— can strengthen your business case for prioritizing well-being.

Stewarding culture

A good starting point is to examine your organization's purpose, values, or cultural principles. While the right words may already be on the page, you can further embed well-being into the storytelling and examples that bring these values to life. Weaving key messages into internal communications reinforces the behaviors desired. One framework to play with is an empathy map[74] that explores what people think, say, feel, or do. In many ways, this exercise allows you to integrate the mind, heart, and body into cultural transformation efforts. By mapping out key experiences, we can make explicit the impact we wish to have. For instance, a company might have trust as a core value. So, if an employee needs to take a few hours off work, we may want them to:

Think: My manager will be understanding.

Say: I need to leave a few hours early on Tuesday. I'll make sure the work is covered. (As opposed to feeling like they need to lie, e.g., I don't feel well, so I am going home.)

Feel: I am so lucky to work at a place with this flexibility.

Do: Tell other colleagues that it's ok to ask for what they need.

While this example may seem very basic, I think it is possibly one of the most common transactions demonstrating the dynamic between trust and well-being. Where are the other small but frequent moments that matter in your organization?

Decision-making is another key area where culture is experienced. Are decisions made by empowered, cross-functional teams, or does everything need approval from top leadership? When a leader gives a command, is the response always "how high?" Do employees have a say in where and how they work? This is a complex issue in many organizations, but offering more flexibility and autonomy at the employee level can help support collective well-being. A simple approach is to regularly ask employees, "What's one thing that could support your autonomy in your role?" There's no need for an extensive process—just a conversation to explore options. If a request can't be accommodated, make sure to explain why. Fostering informal dialogue around decision-making helps create a culture of feedback, openness, and transparency.

Leadership plays a crucial role in shaping corporate culture. A supportive manager can significantly influence employee well-being in various ways. However, a recent SHRM study[75] revealed a notable gap between how leadership and employees perceive the company's impact on mental health. "Leaders and workers have quite different mental health experiences: Nine in 10 human resource and C-suite leaders surveyed said that working for their company had a positive impact on employee mental health, while only half of employees agreed." One of the most crucial decisions a company can make is defining its expectations for managers. Equally important is holding them accountable to those standards, especially during challenging times, as that's when employees will truly trust the leadership. What's remarkable about setting clear expectations for good leadership is that once a tipping point is reached, even new managers instinctively know how to act because the behavior becomes ingrained in the company culture.

While leaders may have different styles, it's helpful to convey consistent messages from the top that employee well-being is a priority. For example, a Chief People Officer shared that their organization analyzes prescription data to monitor any increases in depression and anxiety medication across their workforce. If any rise is observed, leaders are provided with tools and guidance to address employee stress and needs during difficult times. This approach not only emphasizes the organization's commitment to employee mental health but also helps reduce the stigma surrounding it. Whether through messaging, decision-making, or leadership expectations, intentionally shaping desired cultural behaviors can strengthen your well-being strategy and drive business impact.

Structuring programs

While strategy and culture may take time and intention, programs often get the most attention. This is not only where actions are most easily communicated to employees, but also where costs can quickly accumulate. While offering targeted wellness programs like yoga and meditation is an obvious option, there are many other ways to foster well-being. For instance, investing in leadership development and training employees on the behaviors discussed in Chapter 7 can be a great starting point. Providing fair and equitable compensation promotes financial well-being, while recognition doesn't need to cost anything—it can be as simple as expressing gratitude at the start of a team meeting. Adjusting performance management criteria from "above and beyond" labels, which encourage overworking, to more thoughtful language can set a healthier tone. Additionally, effective organizational design and workforce planning can support sustainable performance by maintaining a balance between demands and resources.

The point is you don't necessarily need to create entirely new initiatives to support collective well-being within your organization. Instead, focus on making small adjustments to what you already have in place to enhance well-being opportunities. For instance, adding "including mental health" to your sick policy can help employees feel comfortable taking a mental health day without having to lie or negotiate, which may ultimately prevent them from needing to take physical sick days. Simplifying or improving communication around existing policies can also be a step forward. A company can set a simple goal of reviewing three to five programs or policies each year, gradually improving efficiency. Remember, progress over perfection usually wins.

Closing

Several years have passed since the peak of the pandemic, yet many companies are still trying to find the balance between employee needs and business needs. Considering the broader context of strategy and culture, companies have a chance to apply a well-being perspective that supports the health and productivity of their employees. The global pandemic may have sparked a remote work revolution, but there's no need to wait for another crisis to prepare for what's next. We all need to figure out the future of work together. Embracing the shift in the employee/employer contract could be key to securing a competitive advantage and the future success of the organization. Choose a direction and begin taking action.

Chapter highlights:

- Leadership obviously casts a big shadow on the collective well-being of an organization, but a single leader can't carry the bag alone. For this chapter, I'm going to level up work-life harmony (more individually modeled) to that of collective well-being and sustainable performance.

- The key elements to align are strategy, culture, and programs. Strategy, in its simplest form, is just a framework for making tradeoff decisions in how we compete. Culture is where strategy comes to life through execution. Programs provide a structural means to support both strategy and an aligned culture.

- Organizational decision-makers may need to review data from various research entities to fully understand the impact of well-being on the bottom line before committing more time and resources to an embedded strategy.

- A good starting point is to examine your organization's purpose, values, or cultural principles. While the right words may already be on the page, you can further embed well-being into the storytelling and examples that bring these values to life. Whether through messaging, decision-making, or leadership expectations, intentionally shaping desired cultural behaviors can strengthen your well-being strategy and drive business impact.

- While strategy and culture may take time and intention, programs often get the most attention. The point is you don't necessarily need to create entirely new initiatives to support collective well-being within your organization. Instead, focus on making small adjustments to what you already have in place to enhance well-being opportunities.

Organizational variables to reflect on:

There can be some low-hanging fruit for organizations to better incorporate well-being. Psychological safety is foundational to almost all of them.

1. Equal pay – While this is being legislated in many places at the time of writing, companies can easily do regular check-ups.

2. Flexible work arrangements – This is currently a hot topic with companies bringing people back to the office full-time. There is still an opportunity to keep these in place, as many organizations offered them before the pandemic.

3. Performance and Recognition programs – Is your recognition program currently rewarding "facetime" or outcomes? Consider recognizing key behaviors like collaboration or values that strengthen the desired culture. Be mindful of language like "above and beyond" that may reinforce overworking or appearing busy.

4. Leadership tools and practices – This is where companies can achieve the greatest ROI in improving well-being. Strong management skills not only drive business results but also enhance employee mental health.

5. DEI – At the time of writing this has become a polarizing topic. If you already have a DEI strategy in place, integrating well-being is a natural next step. If not, you can work on both simultaneously, as they complement and strengthen each other. Remember, SHRM's data[76] shows that "workers who feel a strong sense of belonging at work are 2.5 times less likely to feel burned out."

6. Layoffs – Be mindful of who gets laid off and the message it conveys. I've seen leadership in Employee Resource Groups gutted, or primarily remote and part-time employees let go. This sends the message that contributing to the organization in diverse ways is not valued or safe.

CHAPTER 10

Formalizing flexible working

"Leaders honor their core values, but they are
flexible in how they execute them."
—Colin Powell.

One of the positive outcomes of the pandemic was that it highlighted how remote and hybrid work does not hinder productivity, dispelling many misconceptions. However, I still hear from many people whose companies are struggling to navigate remote and hybrid work options—or have simply reverted to a five-day office workweek. While there's no one-size-fits-all solution, I believe organizations that embrace flexible working will ultimately win the long-term game in attracting and retaining talent. The key is trusting employees to shape the path to their best and most sustainable performance. This could start with establishing a formal flexible work arrangement process and policy, but even without a defined program, there are still ways to implement flexible work options that benefit both the organization and its employees.

In this chapter, I hope to guide you in devising a proposal to support the most work-life harmony for yourself. In terms of formal arrangements, here are the commonly used options to consider, flexing time and/or location:

1. Flex time: Typically, the employee picks their start and end times, e.g., 6 am – 2 pm vs. 9 am – 5 pm. Usually connected with in-office work.

2. Core hours: Employees can work their hours of choosing, but those must include core hours, e.g., 10 am – 2 pm, to allow for overlap with other employees. Location may or may not be agnostic here.

3. Hybrid: Probably the most well-known, but this is usually flexibility in location—for example, 3 days in the office and 2 days working from home.

4. Remote: The employee does not come into the office and works from a different location, typically from home.

5. Part-time: Usually reduced hours for reduced pay, most commonly 24/32 hour or three/four-day weeks.

6. Compressed work week: These schedules usually work around 40-hour weeks but may be compressed into fewer days. The most common are 40:10 (10-hour days) or 9:80 (1 day off every two weeks, expecting the extra hours to get spread across the other 9 days).

7. 4-day work week: 100% productivity, 100% pay, 80% hours. It is important to note this is about working less hours but at the same pay.

8. Job sharing: Two people share the workload and outcome expectations of one job. This will usually result in something similar to part-time. Location may or may not be agnostic here.

As you explore your favored options, you may want to consider whether your needs are short-term (1 year or less), long-term (12 months or more), or transitional (typically as a bridge to retirement or to support a successor). Some options may also have financial impacts on you or the organization. While it may not happen overnight, you can certainly keep using some of the tools in this book to support a future transition.

Creating a win-win plan

When reflecting on your purpose for work, it can be helpful to ground yourself in the personal reasons you want a flexible schedule. This can serve as a reminder on days when you feel disheartened or disconnected. For example, after the first year of the pandemic, with two elementary-aged children attending school only a few hours a day, I realized how important it was to have the flexibility of a couple of full days off each week. This allowed me to better prioritize my role as a mother, as well as make time for self-care, mindfulness, and relationships. Understanding my purpose, needs, and identities enabled me to be intentional about where I focused my energy.

When my company introduced part-time options, I had to create a proposal that would not only appeal to my manager but also gain support from other leaders. Thankfully, we had a strong working relationship, and I knew he was a creative problem solver with a progressive mindset. Having been with the company for several years in different roles, I understood how my skills could align with the organization's needs. I presented him with at least four or five potential options, and we collaborated to find the most feasible solution. The final plan required me to stay in my current job until a replacement was found. It took about six months to transition from my HR Business Partner role to one focused mainly on strategic enterprise projects. I share this experience to offer a glimpse into one possible journey.

I hope that my win-win mindset played a role in securing approval for my transition to part-time. I was committed to continuing to contribute meaningfully to the organization, utilizing my business knowledge, skills, and network to deliver great results. I provided clear examples of how this arrangement could benefit the business. At the same time, I approached the conversation with a spirit of co-creation, emphasizing my flexibility and willingness to collaborate with my boss on the terms. We both understood that this might not be a permanent arrangement, but it met a crucial need in my life at that moment. Ultimately, honoring work-life harmony is about navigating the different stages and phases of life and understanding how work fits into the bigger picture. I am incredibly grateful for the opportunity I had and even more delighted to share my learning with you.

The hidden biases of flexible working

While flexible working offers significant benefits for both employees and organizations, it can also expose individuals to common unconscious biases in the workplace. These biases affect everyone, and simply being in a different building or floor can still make you susceptible to them. The key is that these biases often remain unconscious until they are brought to light. Here are some to watch out for:

Proximity bias – This tendency occurs when people in positions of power or leadership tend to favor those who are physically closer to them. In general, there is a vibe of "If I can't see you working, then you must not be working." Additionally, some leaders may simply feel more comfortable knowing you're readily available when they need you. Being unavailable some days of the week makes it hard to meet that need for the leader, especially when they want to be respectful of your flexible schedule. So that may mean that the cool new project goes to another colleague instead of you. These are the times to remember your purpose, especially if you had been a very integrated member of a team before moving to a flexible arrangement. You may have to remind people that you can work flexibly and attend the occasional meeting on off days or rearrange your schedule if that suits you. Or just be okay with it!

Affinity bias – This is an inclination to gravitate toward people who share similar interests, backgrounds, and experiences. If the weekly team lunch or monthly happy hour falls on a day you're not scheduled to work, it's perfectly fine to skip it. However, if you're not putting in enough effort to connect with colleagues, you may find yourself being overlooked. As discussed earlier, maintaining an active network when you're available can help you stay in the loop.

Attribution bias – This is the tendency to attribute a person's behavior to their character or personality rather than considering situational factors. I'll admit, this one is especially triggering for me. I've always prided myself on being a hard worker. At one point during my part-time journey, I was considering returning to full-time work as my kids were older, back in school, and involved in activities. I wanted more professional development and challenge. While exploring a full-time opportunity with an executive, she mentioned, "Well, it won't be a cushy job." I must have made a face because she quickly backtracked, but that's when it hit me: part-time work can be unfairly associated with laziness or lack of commitment. Despite my proven work ethic, my part-time status possibly branded me. This bias can apply to any flexible work arrangement as well.

Some of these biases may be difficult to confront or navigate, but there are always steps you can take. Many of my colleagues knew how to leverage my skills effectively, and I was able to contribute and collaborate with them easily. Others respected my schedule but needed occasional reminders that it was always okay to ask for help, and I would be transparent about whether I could take on additional tasks based on my workload. While I always strived to add value, there were times I felt underutilized. It often surprised me that companies would invest millions in part-time external consultants yet struggle to maximize the potential of their own internal resources. These biases can also make you more vulnerable to layoffs. I share this to encourage you to enter a flexible work arrangement with eyes wide open. If you encounter issues that might cross into legally protected areas, I recommend discussing them with your manager, HR, Employee Relations, or an ombudsperson.

Job crafting around your needs

Job crafting is the process by which employees shape their roles to better align with their needs, interests, and strengths. In my case, my part-time schedule consisted of 24 hours, typically spread over three days a week. As an exempt employee, I wasn't eligible for overtime, so I didn't need to track hours meticulously. However, the structure of working three days a week helped me manage my workaholic tendencies and set clear expectations. I had friends who also worked a part-time schedule, and we all had different experiences. The key is to design the role and tasks around the agreed-upon work hours. Some people may shift to part-time only to find that they are doing the same amount of work for less pay. There are legalities to this that both employees and employers should be mindful of to avoid potential discrimination. If the workload isn't adjusted or boundaries aren't respected, a person isn't truly working part-time—they're simply being taken advantage of. It may take some trial and error, but open, transparent communication is essential for job crafting to find the right balance between workload and outcomes.

This is where the skills we've discussed earlier can really come into play. Setting clear boundaries and being intentional about maintaining them is a key form of support. For many of us, this is one of the most challenging aspects. By understanding your needs and discussing the conditions for success with your manager, you can better plan and prioritize your efforts. Expanding your network and learning about your colleagues' developmental goals can also help when sharing or transitioning tasks to others who can benefit from them. Try documenting a typical week to assess how you're spending your time. Record the tasks, meetings, and relational activities, then review them critically to identify what supports your most valuable work and what may be hindering your progress.

You can also experiment with your schedule to see what works best for you. A former colleague shared that he was about to reach his vacation accrual limit, so he decided to take every Monday and Friday off for a month. He described it as one of the most productive, creative, and rejuvenating work months he'd ever had. You don't need to be at your vacation max to try something similar, though. You could experiment with a four-day week or a three-day week. Pay attention to how you feel physically, emotionally, and mentally using your mindfulness skills. Observe the results and see what could be sustained through job crafting. If you find that you're more productive and can demonstrate this in a short experiment, it could increase your chances of getting your flexible work proposal approved.

If you're job hunting, another strategy is to pitch a flexible work arrangement during the recruitment process. I've had friends mention that a job they were considering didn't meet their salary expectations. Depending on the company and your financial situation, this could be a chance to propose a reduced schedule that aligns with their budget to the hiring manager. This approach allows you to work fewer hours while staying within their salary range, creating a budget-neutral solution. This could be appealing to a growing startup, for example, which might be open to hiring a senior-level employee part-time with the possibility of transitioning to full-time as the company expands.

This approach could even benefit the organization financially by avoiding costly recruiting or consultant fees in the future. While there are many factors to consider, this is just another example of how job crafting can create win-win situations.

Navigating the nuts and bolts

It's important to be aware of the broader impacts on the system and organization when transitioning to a flexible work arrangement. In some cases, you may need to consult with Human Resources, as a redesign of the organization could be necessary. Your role and responsibilities may need to be adjusted, along with potential changes to your compensation. Another possible outcome is that a colleague who takes on some of your previous duties may receive a promotion (and remember to celebrate their success, as you're achieving your own goals too). Alternatively, your organization might need to add a new headcount to support the changes in workload. If your company offers job-sharing as a primary part-time option, you may need to find a partner to share your role. There can be a ripple effect from these changes that could impact the approval process, feasibility, and timing of your flexible work proposal. The more carefully you consider these factors, the stronger your proposal will be.

The 4-day work week is also starting to gain popularity in many Western countries[77]. This model offers the same pay for the same level of productivity but with fewer and more thoughtfully prioritized hours. Legislation around this is also evolving, so it's worth keeping an eye on any developments in your country or state, especially if it's not yet in place. It's important to distinguish this approach from compressed workweek schedules, as achieving the same work in less time will require working differently. This approach should still align with maintaining your work-life harmony, so it's crucial to ensure that the reduced hours don't compromise your well-being.

If your need for a flexible work schedule is temporary, such as due to caregiving responsibilities, you might want to explore a leave of absence. A leave provides a temporary break while preserving your employment status and often retaining other benefits. Instead of taking a full-time leave, you may also have the option for intermittent or reduced schedule leave. Reach out to your Human Resources department to discuss the best options for your situation.

Closing

Flexible working may sound dreamy, but it is not for everyone. There can be a financial and possible career hit. People may assume you are out of the rat race. When used well, flexible working also doesn't need to be a forever thing. It can suit a specific time in life, such as caregiving for children or aging parents, helping with a family business transition, healing from an illness, preparing to be in a marathon, or working on a side hustle. While the purpose behind it doesn't matter, some reasons will be more socially sanctioned than others for sure. Crafting a proposal that makes a concrete win-win for both you and the organization will be important, as will maintaining open lines of communication.

Your network matters. Consider how to get colleagues on board with your flexible work arrangement. You may also need to manage your reputation and personal brand to ensure your arrangement remains successful. Flexible work arrangements shouldn't be a new means of quiet quitting, but rather the invigorating option to keep you contributing sustainably. Don't ruin it for others, man! Keep the win-win mindset so flexible work can be a viable option for all.

Before proposing a flexible work arrangement, consider what tasks you can realistically delegate or take off your plate during the reduced hours. If a salary adjustment is necessary, weigh the trade-offs carefully. It might also be helpful to experiment with new work habits before committing to the change. Many people are so skilled at their jobs that they can achieve excellent results in four days while still getting paid for full-time work. If that's the case for you, you might not need this book—you've probably already figured out your work-life harmony!

Chapter highlights:

- The key success factor in flexible work arrangements is that companies trust their employees to create the path to their best and most sustainable performance. There are at least eight commonly used arrangements to consider.

- A win-win mindset may play a role in securing approval of a flexible work arrangement. Whatever the proposal, committed employees can continue adding value to the organization, leveraging their business knowledge, skills, and network to deliver great results.

- While flexible working offers significant benefits for both employees and organizations, it can also expose individuals to common unconscious biases in the workplace. These biases affect everyone, and simply being in a different building or floor can still make you susceptible to them. The key is that these biases often remain unconscious until they are brought to light.

- Job crafting is a process where employees design their jobs to better fit their needs, interests, and strengths. The key factor is crafting the role and tasks to be accomplished in the proposed work hours. There are many ways to experiment with job crafting.
- It is also helpful to be aware of the system and organization impacts that may result from shifting to a flexible work arrangement. Human Resources and your manager will be your primary partners in navigating the possibilities. Flexible work arrangements shouldn't be a new means of quiet quitting, but rather can be the invigorating option to keep you contributing sustainably.

And...ACTION! Simple tools and practices to play with:

1. Reflect back on your purpose(s) captured from the thought starters in the previous chapters. If everything goes right, what can be gained from transitioning to a flexible work arrangement? If everything goes wrong, what will keep you grounded in navigating any trade-offs?

2. Experiment with a win-win proposal. Some ideas to consider incorporating:

   a. Your strengths and interests, combined with your knowledge of the business.

    b. Triple constraints of project management: Is there scope that can be impacted? Time or money that can be saved? Quality that can be enhanced?

    c. Consider the concerns of your teammates, manager, and partners. How can you ensure they are comfortable and know how to leverage you appropriately?

3. Start tracking your days for a week or more—notice times when you feel happy and energized, activities you tolerate, and tasks that drive you crazy. Leverage the great job crafting[78] resources on positivepsychology.com.

4. Schedule regular check-in meetings or "sync sessions" with your team or key coworkers to share updates on your projects and initiatives. Use this time to provide a quick overview of what you're working on, your current capacity, and any support you might need. Similarly, listen to others' updates to understand their priorities and find opportunities to collaborate or align efforts. This ongoing communication ensures visibility, relevance, and balanced workloads across the team.

5. Revisit your boundaries. What are deal-breakers, and where can you stay flexible?

6. Practice getting clear on conditions of success or outcomes. Notice where you might be busy for busy's sake as opposed to working toward a clear result or purpose. As you shift to some flexible work arrangements, you may need to be more intentional about working differently.

CHAPTER 11

Empowering the future and going deeper

"Every time you are tempted to react in the same old way, ask if you want to be a prisoner of the past or a pioneer of the future."
—Deepak Chopra.

Whether you're looking to take steps for your own work-life harmony or contribute to the broader well-being movement, there are countless options to explore. This book provides a starting point, but many of you may want to dive deeper into certain areas and truly enhance your efforts. Below are some recommendations for additional resources and support.

How can Human Resources (HR) help?

I have worked with a lot of wonderful HR people who really do want to help employees. Your HR partner can be a great coach and thought partner, but they may not be able to do everything you think they can. Per the previous chapters, HR can help you brainstorm some potential options or connect you with resources like a leave of absence if needed.

What about coaching?

Coaching, whether individual or group, can be especially effective in helping you break free from feeling stuck. Future-focused coaches help guide you in planning actionable steps to reach your goals. Coaches may specialize in different areas. For instance, as an integral coach, I work with clients holistically, considering their entire life experience to help them increase their capacity to stay present and align with their purpose and context. On the other hand, some coaches may focus more on performance goals and skill development. It's important to find a coach who aligns with your needs and feels like a trusted partner.

When working with individual clients, I often guide them through many of the same exercises outlined in this book. However, coaching adds an extra layer of accountability, partnership, and personalized support to help drive meaningful change. Group coaching offers these same benefits while also fostering a sense of community, enabling participants to share habits and practices and gain insights from others' experiences. Ideal clients are those ready to embrace change and committed to achieving specific goals. They may have experimented with new approaches before but struggled to sustain them. Coaching provides the tools and support to help you overcome obstacles and move forward in transformative ways.

How do we support work toward collective well-being?

As discussed in earlier chapters, there are many ways to create an organization that empowers individuals to achieve their ideal work-life harmony. Depending on your goals and level of commitment, you can collaborate with professionals like me to provide organization development consulting, skill-building workshops, or tailored advising. Additionally, leveraging the influence of affinity groups or employee resource groups can be a powerful way to initiate change. Inviting me or similar experts for speaking engagements can help spark meaningful discussions and inspire new ideas within your organization. And for a list of organizations that are also working toward collective well-being, go to my website, www.workinghelltoworkingwell.com.

What other resources do you recommend?

There are countless books, articles, podcasts, and other resources to support you. Leverage the notes section to find some helpful ones.

Conclusion

"Those who have an opportunity to work in organizations that treat them like human beings to be protected rather than a resource to be exploited come home at the end of the day with an intense feeling of fulfillment and gratitude. This should be the rule for all of us, not the exception. Returning from work feeling inspired, safe, fulfilled and grateful is a natural human right to which we are all entitled and not a modern luxury that only a few lucky ones are able to find." —Simon Sinek.

Thank you for allowing me to be part of your journey. I am deeply grateful that you've stayed with me through to the end. Whether you've skimmed through and picked up a practice or two or read every word, I hope you've found something valuable. Most importantly, take a moment to express gratitude to yourself for taking even the smallest steps toward investing in your well-being.

This book started from a place of care and concern for how people are working in Corporate America. I truly believe there is a place between the extremes of working ourselves sick and being sick of working where we can make work meaningful and sustainable again. In my words, that would be called work-life harmony. No matter the hours I work, I am able to hold both beliefs that 1) I am fully committed to my job/work/organization AND 2) This is just part of who I am, and I can make space for other people/activities/hobbies that make me feel alive. I can flow between work and life demands as needs arise. The path from hustle to harmony starts with taking action, no matter how small, to let our bodies feel this new way of being.

It begins with recognizing what it means for you to courageously show up as your whole self at work and assessing how safe it feels to do so. Practicing mindfulness in your heart, body, and mind helps you stay present and aware of what is unfolding in the moment. These practices enable you to approach situations with intention, choosing how to respond rather than reacting automatically. Additionally, clarifying your sense of purpose—or even multiple purposes—provides greater clarity and alignment by guiding your focus and actions toward what truly matters to you.

As we begin to observe more of our inner world, we can start to notice how the stories we tell ourselves may fuel cycles of self-talk that reinforce workaholic tendencies. These patterns can leave us feeling overwhelmed, stuck, and too time-poor to make meaningful changes. However, by exploring the fears that often keep us trapped in these habits, we can start to reclaim More Time Now. For example, fear of inadequacy may prompt behaviors like overpreparing and overperforming because "More is better," right? Similarly, a fear of failure may lead to setting unrealistic standards or avoiding asking for help, perpetuating the feeling that "I don't have enough time." Or a fear of rejection may keep us in a cycle of responsiveness and over-commitment, whereby we can't escape the urgent need to "do it now." Fortunately, evidence-based strategies can help us shift from these cortisol- and adrenaline-fueled fear states—whether they manifest as fight, flight, or freeze—and move us toward a place of greater calm, clarity, and control.

Reducing harmful stress levels and achieving a state of greater well-being is an important goal. The journey begins by identifying what matters most and envisioning the behaviors that align with that future state. Since work is often a social and collaborative space, understanding our social-emotional needs can help us shape a work experience that feels fulfilling and aligned with our life vision. It doesn't have to be perfect—simply meeting more of our core needs can foster greater resilience and satisfaction.

By recognizing our various identities, we can also reflect on the habits that reinforce them and explore new ways to express ourselves. At times, our identities or values may conflict, creating internal tension. Developing awareness of these tensions can help us navigate tradeoffs or uncover new solutions that promote a sense of balance and harmony in both our personal and professional lives.

Through self-reflection, supported by mindfulness or the prompts in this book, we can begin examining how our behaviors manifest, starting with our habits—those often subconscious, automated patterns. Building awareness of these habits and identifying opportunities to form new, intentional ones is a powerful way to practice new ways of being. To support these shifts, it's essential to explore how we generate and sustain energy. While adrenaline can provide a quick boost, relying on it excessively can harm our well-being. Instead, we can focus on cultivating creative, connection, and completion energy throughout our day for a more balanced and sustainable approach to productivity. Equally important is maintaining strong boundaries to protect the energy we create, ensuring it isn't drained by activities or interactions that don't align with our priorities or needs.

Once you've identified the behaviors you want to build on, you can prepare to take action using the 3Ps: Planning, Pacing, and Playing. Start with a plan—it doesn't need to be overly detailed or elaborate. Simplicity often works best. Focus on one clear, manageable step or action you can take right away. More isn't always better, remember? Next, consider your pacing. How often should you take this action? Is it something to try once a day, three times a week, or perhaps just once a month? Experiment and play with different rhythms to find what feels right, realistic, and sustainable for you. Lastly, be kind to yourself as you move forward. Remember, progress takes time. Embrace a growth mindset and remind yourself that you're not there *yet*, but you're on your way. Feeling empowered in your choices will help you stay engaged and confident as you interact with others and continue to build momentum.

Creating meaningful change in your life often requires support. Identifying your supportive core—those who can act as cheerleaders and truth-tellers—can help you stay aligned with your goals. Expanding your network is equally important, as it not only strengthens your ability to adopt work-life harmony but also allows you to model the well-being that comes with it. A strong, cross-functional network ensures you stay informed about organizational priorities, enabling you to plan and pace your work more effectively. When you understand what matters to others, there is always room to negotiate. While this may require some courageous experimentation, reframing situations and advocating clearly for your needs can pave the way for you—and those around you—to work more sustainably.

People leaders play a crucial role in modeling and enabling work-life harmony for their teams. To effectively support others, it's essential to start with yourself, ensuring you have the capacity and capability to lead by example. The good news? It doesn't require learning brand-new skills—just a focused intention to sharpen core management practices. One of the most impactful skills is talent development, both at the individual and team levels. This doesn't have to be time-intensive, as you can leverage other resources to support growth. Think of it as the ultimate team sport! Providing clarity on what success looks like—both in outcomes and collaboration with you—helps build trust and foster open communication. When engaging with your team, be mindful of the inherent power dynamic. Negotiating workload or work practices can require significant courage on their part. Showing empathy for their motivations and concerns creates a supportive environment. This approach not only helps your team feel valued but also boosts engagement and performance—making you look like an exceptional leader in the process!

While we've captured a lot of what leaders and individuals can do based on the assumption that many companies are just not wired for well-being yet, there are always options at the organizational level. Embedding well-being into the company's strategy, culture, and programs offers various levers for people and organizations to pull, depending on the level of commitment and investment. There's substantial evidence linking a healthy workforce to improved bottom lines and other positive outcomes. Organizations can also tap into their own data—such as surveys and crowdsourced metrics—to inform their approach.

An employee well-being strategy can be seamlessly integrated into broader organizational strategies in many companies. However, this strategy alone isn't enough without a cultural framework to support how work is done. Leadership and decision-making are likely already places infused with cultural nuance, so adding an intention around well-being can have a big impact. Well-being programs also provide a structural foundation for organizations to support their employees. This book is all about small, actionable changes, and the same concept applies at the organizational level. Just as individuals benefit from aligning attention with intention, so too can organizations achieve sustainable performance by focusing on well-being.

For those looking to take the next step and actually work a flexible schedule, I've shared some insights from my own experience. While a part-time schedule certainly helped curb my workaholic tendencies, it came with its own set of challenges. I've discussed some unconscious biases you may encounter and key factors to consider when proposing a flexible work arrangement. You can start by job crafting your role, experimenting with responsibilities, productivity, and scheduling. By using the reflections and tools you've already learned, you can create a win-win situation for both you and the organization.

This book was designed to get you into action, transforming those "shoulds" into real possibilities. However, I understand that some of you may still be seeking deeper insight. Fortunately, there's no shortage of resources, and you're not alone. On the people side, you have access to managers, mentors, HR partners, coaches, family, friends, and others for support. Additionally, there are many resources available, from articles and books to podcasts and well-being apps. Recognizing that you have options is the first crucial step.

And for getting this far in your journey, I want to share one last mini model with you. Like any corporate veteran, I love a good acronym. If you walk away from this book with just one new way of working, I hope it is embracing the power of the P.A.U.S.E:

P: Pause – No matter the situation, when you are feeling triggered, confused, emotional, or any other curious bodily sensation, know that there is always time for at least a short pause. Whether that is noticing your breathing or using a simple statement like, "I'm processing what you said. Can I have a few seconds to think more deeply about that?" you have the power to create space for yourself.

A: Allow – Many of us get stuck in a cycle of resisting our emotions or sensations. Try staying curious and see what unfolds when you simply allow them to be.

U: Understand – As you continue practicing, you'll begin to notice behaviors connected to your values, habits, or identity, for instance. This is the beautiful part of gaining deeper self-awareness, allowing you to make choices that align more closely with your purpose.

S: Smile – You've got this!

E: Empathize – There will always be good days, bad days, and everything in between. Show yourself some self-compassion, and extend empathy to others who likely didn't wake up with a plan to annoy you but managed to, nonetheless.

My original purpose in writing this book was to help you find at least a few more hours for living, not just working. I started this journey with deep concern about the state of work today, but I finished with hope and optimism. Just as our current ways of working led us to this point, I also believe work can be the path out of this predicament. It can be a space where we discover our strengths, find meaning and purpose, and support our livelihoods. Work can also foster connections and meaningful relationships, helping to tackle the loneliness epidemic. By working together, leveraging our collective strengths and diverse perspectives, we have the power to solve the world's greatest challenges and create a brighter, more sustainable future for all.

I wish you the gift of work-life harmony, where you can share your talents with the world while also making time for what brings you joy. May you "Leave Loudly" as much as possible. And I hope you find inner peace with whatever choices you pursue. Change can be daunting, and your inner critic may argue, "This isn't what keeps us safe." But, YOU. ARE. NOT. ALONE. The more of us who embrace this new way of working, the more we'll begin to see change in the world around us. Join me in the well-being movement!

The world needs us.

Acknowledgements

To my husband, Erik, thank you for your unwavering support while I embarked on this new chapter. You are my rock, and I wouldn't be able to do taxes without you. In all seriousness, you have been my best life decision.

To Tucker and Tessa: Thank you for being some of my greatest teachers. May you continue uncovering your hidden talents and share them boldly with the world. You are my pride and joy.

To my parents, Harold and Marjorie, it is hard to know where to begin in expressing my gratitude for the lifelong support of following my dreams. This book would not exist without your unconditional love.

To Dara, the sister who is the envy of all sisters. We complete each other's sentences, which I should have realized much earlier in the book writing process. Thank you for being a giant part of my support system. I would not be me without you.

To Terra and Barbara, my soul sisters, thank you for your enduring friendship from such an early age. Your ability to leave the world better than you found it inspires me endlessly, and I love seeing the way community flourishes around you.

To my Cal Girls (Anne, Carrie, Dana, Jen, Kelli and Marisa), your friendship nourishes me through all of life's ups and downs. I am humbled to be in the company of such changemakers and (sometimes) former hellraisers. Our shared journeys through life, parenthood, and careers are woven into these pages. A heartfelt thanks to Kelli for being my greatest role model on this author's path and for letting me ride your coattails and follow in your footsteps.

To the McBarte Clan, our celebrations of life are soul affirming. As the saying goes, friends are the family you choose for yourselves. Thank you for always seeing me.

To my amazing clients, your stories have inspired so much of this book. Thank you for honoring me with your trust, your pain, your gifts, your challenges, your patience and your curiosity. I have grown so much from our partnership.

To the many friends, colleagues, classmates, leaders, managers, and mentors who have been part of my supportive core—I'm deeply grateful for each of you. There are too many to name, but I hope you know who you are. Thank you for being teachers, guides and partners on my journey thus far. I hope we continue to grow and play together.

Notes

[1] https://worldhappinesssummit.com/about/

[2] https://globalwellnessinstitute.org/what-is-wellness/

[3] https://www.webmdhealthservices.com/blog/wellness-vs-well-being-whats-the-difference/#:~:text=Navigating%20the%20blurring%20of%20home,recognize%20one's%20overall%20health%20situation.

[4] https://wellbeing.hmc.ox.ac.uk/news/more-ambition-needed-to-improve-workplace-wellbeing/

[5] https://wellbeing.hmc.ox.ac.uk/news/more-ambition-needed-to-improve-workplace-wellbeing/

[6] https://www.indeed.com/lead/new-research-work-wellbeing-is-good-for-people-and-profits

[7] https://www.shrm.org/topics-tools/news/inclusion-diversity/burnout-shrm-research-2024

[8] https://www.who.int/news/item/28-05-2019-burn-out-an-occupational-phenomenon-international-classification-of-diseases#:~:text=Burn%2Dout%20is%20defined%20in,in%20other%20areas%20of%20life.%E2%80%9D

[9] https://www.cnn.com/2023/09/14/health/gen-z-mental-health-gallup-wellness-cec/index.html?utm_source=link_wwwv9&utm_campaign=item_544712&utm_medium=copy

[10] https://www.bbc.com/worklife/article/20171003-proof-that-people-have-always-complained-about-young-adults

[11] https://culturepartners.com/landing-page/employee-fulfillment-ebook/

[12] https://lifestance.com/blog/is-gen-z-the-most-stressed-generation/

[13] https://www.stress.org/workplace-stress/

[14] https://www.apa.org/news/press/releases/stress/2023/collective-trauma-recovery

[15] https://abcnews.go.com/Health/us-surgeon-general-warns-dangers-loneliness/story?id=111050040

16 https://hbr.org/2017/06/burnout-at-work-isnt-just-about-exhaustion-its-also-about-loneliness

17 https://www.shrm.org/topics-tools/news/inclusion-diversity/burnout-shrm-research-2024

18 Clark, M. (2024). *Never not working*. Boston, MA: Harvard Business Review Press.

19 https://www.forbes.com/sites/rodgerdeanduncan/2024/02/20/are-you-a-workaholic-dont-wear-it-as-a-badge-of-honor/?sh=5875dd2e49fe

20 https://milkeninstitute.org/article/decouple-people-productivity-idea

21 https://www.gallup.com/workplace/236366/right-culture-not-employee-satisfaction.aspx

22 https://leadchangegroup.com/the-key-to-sustainable-performance/

23 https://dwfgroup.com/en/news-and-insights/insights/2024/1/ct24-employee-activism-is-on-the-rise

24 https://www.wilmarschaufeli.nl/publications/Schaufeli/530.pdf

25 Robbins, M. (2018). *Bring your whole self to work*. Carlsbad, CA: Hay House.

26 https://neuroleadership.com/your-brain-at-work/psychological-safety-and-accountability-insights-from-amy-edmondson

27 Kabat-Zinn, J. (2016). *Mindfulness for beginners*. Louisville, CO: Sounds True.

28 David, S. (2016). *Emotional agility*. Avery Publishing Group.

29 https://www.mindfulcoachingtools.com/free-tools/p/the-feelings-wheel

30 https://www.forbes.com/sites/jeroenkraaijenbrink/2018/12/19/what-does-vuca-really-mean/

31 https://www.gallup.com/cliftonstrengths/en/252137/home.aspx

32 https://www.forbes.com/sites/rodgerdeanduncan/2024/02/20/are-you-a-workaholic-dont-wear-it-as-a-badge-of-honor/?sh=5875dd2e49fe

33 Goleman, D. (2007). *Emotional Intelligence* (10th ed.). New York, NY: Bantam Books.

34 https://www.simplypsychology.org/amygdala-hijack.html#:~:text=Daniel%20Goleman%20first%20coined%20the%20term%20amygdala

35 https://www.mayoclinic.org/healthy-lifestyle/stress-management/in-depth/stress/art-20046037?p=

[36] https://www.cdc.gov/emotional-wellbeing/features/reduce-stress.htm#print

[37] https://conscious.is/concepts/leading-and-living-from-your-whole-body-yes

[38] https://www.simplypsychology.org/maslow.html

[39] https://neuroleadership.com/research/tools/nli-scarf-assessment/

[40] https://www.cnvc.org/store/feelings-and-needs-inventory

[41] https://www.cnvc.org/store/feelings-and-needs-inventory

[42] https://www.discprofile.com/what-is-disc#:~:text=DiSC%20is%20an%20acronym%20that,on%20accomplishing%20bottom%2Dline%20results.

[43] https://www.insights.com/us/

[44] https://nvcacademy.com/media/NVCA/learning-tools/NVCA-feelings-needs.pdf

[45] https://www.gallup.com/cliftonstrengths/en/252137/home.aspx

[46] Clear, J. (2018). *Atomic habits*. Avery Publishing Group.

[47] https://jamesclear.com/quote/atomic-habits

[48] Rubin, G. (2017). *The four tendencies*. Harmony.

[49] https://gretchenrubin.com/four-tendencies/

[50] Buckingham, M. (2022). *Love + work*. Boston, MA: Harvard Business Review Press.

[51] https://theenergyproject.com/

[52] https://theenergyproject.com/approach/

[53] https://www.facebook.com/brenebrown/posts/heres-what-ive-learned-about-creativity-from-the-world-of-wholehearted-living-an/2025826304099135/

[54] Magsamen, S., & Ross, I. (2023). *Your brain on art*. New York, NY: Random House International.

[55] https://www.theguardian.com/sport/2010/jul/18/team-sky-tour-de-france

[56] https://www.digitalwellnessinstitute.com/?srsltid=AfmBOopOtiSO3n3SJRXdFjNZD6G6msgP5IhOpn944XqjVnwIIpjc2Hy7

[57] https://www.forbes.com/sites/amyblankson/2023/10/03/overcoming-digital-burnout-a-blueprint-for-digital-wellness-at-work/?sh=25234b3a14f5

58 https://www.wgu.edu/blog/what-is-growth-mindset-8-steps-develop-one1904.html#:~:text=Dweck%20says%2C%20%E2%80%9CThis%20growth%20mindset,grow%20through%20application%20and%20experience.%E2%80%9D

59 https://www.cnn.com/2021/04/01/health/stress-good-for-you-wellness/index.html

60 https://www.forbes.com/councils/forbescoachescouncil/2023/06/22/why-and-how-to-practice-the-beginners-mindset/

61 https://medium.com/@jordan/the-five-minute-favor-unleashing-the-power-of-small-acts-of-giving-c4ad3ff9c1f1

62 https://www.facebook.com/appletv/videos/ted-lasso-apple-tv/265531348745828/

63 https://hbr.org/2023/05/more-than-50-of-managers-feel-burned-out

64 https://www.mckinsey.com/capabilities/people-and-organizational-performance/our-insights/the-boss-factor-making-the-world-a-better-place-through-workplace-relationships

65 Maxwell, J. C. (2007). *The 21 irrefutable laws of leadership*. Nashville, TN: Thomas Nelson.

66 https://worldwellbeingmovement.org/playbook/

67 https://wellbeing.hmc.ox.ac.uk/news/more-ambition-needed-to-improve-workplace-wellbeing/

68 https://news.airbnb.com/airbnb-unveils-roadmap-to-bring-magical-travel-to-everyone/

69 https://www.indeed.com/employers/work-wellbeing?gad_source=1&gclid=Cj0KCQjw0ruyBhDuARIsANSZ3wqqqH_mG6MC_TPAMqr1rcj9bEVWtaq8mJ_SjsVy8jfLf3UqelROKqcaAleFEALw_wcB&aceid=&gclsrc=aw.ds

70 https://worldwellbeingmovement.org/

71 https://www.4dayweek.com/

72 https://www.healthyplacetowork.com/

73 https://www.indeed.com/employers/work-wellbeing?gad_source=1&gclid=Cj0KCQjw0ruyBhDuARIsANSZ3wqqqH_mG6MC_TPAMqr1rcj9bEVWtaq8mJ_SjsVy8jfLf3UqelROKqcaAleFEALw_wcB&aceid=&gclsrc=aw.ds

74 https://www.nngroup.com/articles/empathy-mapping/

[75] https://www.shrm.org/topics-tools/news/employee-relations/report-managers-bigger-impact-employee-mental-health-therapists

[76] https://www.shrm.org/topics-tools/news/inclusion-diversity/burnout-shrm-research-2024

[77] https://4dayweek.io/countries

[78] https://positivepsychology.com/job-crafting/

www.ingramcontent.com/pod-product-compliance
Lightning Source LLC
Chambersburg PA
CBHW071418210326
41597CB00020B/3562